W9-AAG-888

PORTER STANSBERRY

AMERICA 2020

VOLUME II

HOW THE RICHEST MEN IN AMERICA ARE PROTECTING THEIR WEALTH RIGHT NOW

About Stansberry Research

Founded in 1999 and based in Baltimore, Maryland, Stansberry Research is an independent subscription-based publisher of financial information, serving millions of investors around the world. Our firm has more than 500,000 paid subscribers in more than 100 countries.

Our business is guided by two simple principles:

1. We strive to give our customers the information we'd want if our roles were reversed.

2. We only publish analysts whose advice and strategies we'd want our own families to read and to follow.

We believe in offering a range of opinions. Experienced analysts with their own unique investment strategies and philosophies lead our brands. As a result, we publish a mosaic of opinions, recommendations, and strategies. This approach gives our work greater breadth, creating more diverse opportunities for our subscribers.

Our analysts are linked, however, by a commitment to risk management and a contrarian approach to identifying investment opportunities. Across all of our franchises, we focus on investments that are unloved, ignored, or unknown. It is in these situations where having an informed perspective gives our subscribers the best risk-to-reward opportunities.

We believe in a long-term approach. Our business strategy is based on building long-term relationships with our customers. We strive to achieve this by providing consistently reliable, actionable, and profitable advice, which creates renewal income for our business. As a result, many of our internal marketing efforts are focused on selling lifetime subscriptions, which give clients access to more (or even all) of our products at a much lower total cost. The same long-term thinking guides the relationships we have with our business partners and our employees.

We believe in transparency and accountability. Sincere goodwill is best demonstrated by routine and reliable measures of performance. We believe that all investment advisers, whether fiduciaries or publishers, should provide an accounting of the outcomes of their advice. All of our investment recommendations are publicly evaluated each year. All of our investment newsletters include a portfolio of open positions in each monthly issue.

We believe in unmatched customer service and no-risk subscriptions. Our overall goal in business is to simply treat our customers as we would like to be treated. When you call our office, we will pick up the phone. And at any time in the first 30 days, if we're unable to meet your expectations for any reason, we are always willing to "part as friends" by promptly refunding your entire subscription fee. There is more than enough risk in the financial world... you will never have to risk a penny buying our products.

Stansberry Research's uncompromised insight has made it one of the most respected and sought-after research organizations in the financial sector. Our analysts have been quoted by the *Wall Street Journal*, *Barron's*, and the *Washington Post*. They have also appeared on major financial news networks, such as Bloomberg and Fox Business News.

Table of Contents

Introduction

More than 350,000 people read our book, *America 2020: The Survival Blueprint*, last year... making it one of the most-read books in the country.

How did a financial publishing firm out of Baltimore, Maryland sell nearly as many books as John Grisham?

Well, we believe the message we spread is that important. And it has struck a chord with concerned Americans at a time when our economy is at its weakest.

Over the past year, we've received hundreds of notes from grateful readers. Here's what just a few had to say...

- *"America 2020: The Survival Blueprint* was outstanding. You put everything in a sequential order that was plain to see and easy to understand." – Mitch K.

- "I devoured *America 2020* and refer to it whenever I am considering an investment." – Leonard A.

- "I have read *America 2020: The Survival Blueprint* four or five times since receiving it last June." – John K.

- *"America 2020* should be required reading for any American." – Shane K.

- "This book was an eye opener for me. I am not a savvy investor and am brand new at the game, but Porter's book encouraged me to learn more." – David W.

- "I read *America 2020*... then I ordered copies for my son and daughters-in-law, my brother, and my secretary. EXCELLENT book!!" – Marilyn G.

- "*America 2020* was the best book of 2015." – Skip M.

In *America 2020: The Survival Blueprint*, we explained how the reckless actions of politicians and central bankers were driving our economy to ruin.

The book was to serve as an owner's manual for how to protect yourself and your family over the next five years.

We partnered with former Texas Congressman and Presidential Candidate Dr. Ron Paul – a man who shares our concerns – to tell the story.

Our goal was to get *America 2020: The Survival Blueprint* into as many homes as possible.

To do that, we created a ridiculous offer.

We only charged folks what it cost us to print and ship the books.

On top of that, we gave anyone who purchased the book a free 30-day trial to our best-selling financial newsletter, *Stansberry's Investment Advisory*.

We knew that rather than telling you about our work, the best thing we could do was to show you the type of research we do, with essentially a free sample.

The response was beyond anything we could have imagined.

If this book had been sold in bookstores or on Amazon, it could have been one of the best-selling nonfiction books of 2015.

Since publishing the original, the economic situation in America has only grown worse...

Seventy percent of investors lost money in 2015.

We've seen nearly $8 trillion disappear from world stock markets.

Even the great Warren Buffett lost money in 2015... $11 billion!

Corporate bond markets have collapsed... and the prices of oil and other commodities such as copper, aluminum, and steel have hit multiyear lows.

Meanwhile, research shows that the top five largest financial institutions (the ones that were bailed out in 2008) are now 25% bigger than they were back then... and more dangerous than ever.

We've seen private businesses take on more debt than at any time in the past 12 years. And an incredible 863 companies had their credit ratings downgraded in 2015... the most since 2009.

Even Wal-Mart announced the shutdown of more than 250 stores worldwide.

We have no doubt that 2016 will mark the emergence of a huge trend of rising debt defaults, falling equity valuations, and commodity liquidation. What's coming is going to be bad – much, much worse than anyone expects.

More debt, lower interest rates, less growth, higher income inequality... And while the situation in America is bleak, it's even worse for the rest of the world.

A strong U.S. dollar and collapsing commodity prices have crushed emerging market economies like Brazil and Venezuela. Growth in Europe is nonexistent. We'll likely see yet another major sovereign default in the near future.

Negative interest rates abound. In fact, **only one-third of global sovereign debt yields higher than 1%**. Savers around the world are being robbed of their hard-earned capital.

While 75 million Baby Boomers worry about protecting their nest egg, the youngest generation may never have a chance to accumulate real wealth. They're saddled with student debt and unable to save enough for a down payment on a house. Stagnant wage growth and a challenging job market make it difficult for this generation to earn a living wage.

At the same time, the youth – and the rest of the world – are waking up to the follies and inevitable boom-and-bust nature of a fiat currency controlled by a central bank.

They're praising characters like Bernie Sanders who, if elected, would raise taxes and redistribute massive amounts of wealth... at a time when the economy couldn't handle such a sudden shift in policy.

So Stansberry Research is back with *America 2020 Volume 2* to tell you about the problems in the economy as we see them today.

In this latest edition, we've gathered the thoughts and opinions of many of the smartest and wealthiest people we know, including...

- One of the most reputable rare-coin and bullion dealers in the country, who has graded and certified about 23 million coins over the last three decades.

- A best-selling author, world-renowned speculator, and libertarian philosopher who is often considered the authority on profiting from periods of turmoil. (He once booked a 59,000% gain on a single trade.)

- An American author, entrepreneur, publisher, real estate investor, filmmaker, and art collector who launched his first business from his kitchen table at age 11.

- And a multimillionaire writer and businessman who is credited with predicting the collapse of the Japanese miracle economy, the fall of the Soviet Union, and the blowup of the dot-com bubble. This man owns hundreds of thousands of acres of land around the world and sees a dozen different business deals cross his desk every single week.

We asked them all one question...

"What problems are you worried about today and what are you doing to protect your wealth?"

My bet is you haven't done much – if anything – to prepare yourself for what lies ahead in America. You've told yourself you should... but it's too complicated to figure out. You don't want to sell stuff that would force you to pay a lot in taxes. Or you figure if you just don't look at your account statement for a while, this will all blow over eventually. You might be right...

Reading *America 2020: The Survival Blueprint* was a critical first step in protecting your wealth.

But there's much, much more you should know about wealth protection than we had room to print in those 300 pages...

We want to give you more.

We've built our business on a simple mission: **To tell our subscribers the information we'd want to know if our roles were reversed.**

It's a simple concept... but it has led us to do things that are profoundly different from what other publishers do.

So the next 280 pages are filled with many ideas and advice from us and our most trusted mentors to see you through the coming crisis in America.

First, you'll read the most up-to-date writings from our founder, Porter Stansberry.

Each section thereafter will focus on writings from one of our expert contacts.

They all answer that pressing question, *"What problems are you worried about today and what are you doing to protect your wealth?"*

You should read this book with a pen and paper close by. You may need to go back two or three times to make sure you've covered everything.

Remember, if you've found yourself reading this book, you understand that we are on the brink of yet another financial crisis in the United States.

What you're about to read is the result of decades of experience in the financial markets. We urge you to take the necessary steps to protect your wealth and your family by educating yourself and playing it smart.

Best regards,

Sean Goldsmith
Managing Director, Stansberry Research

Porter Stansberry

Porter Stansberry founded Stansberry Research in 1999 with the firm's flagship newsletter, *Stansberry's Investment Advisory*.

Prior to launching Stansberry Research, Porter was the first American editor of the *Fleet Street Letter*, the world's oldest English-language financial newsletter.

Today, Porter is well-known for doing some of the most important – and often controversial – work in the financial-advisory business. Since he launched *Stansberry's Investment Advisory*, his string of accurate forecasts has made his newsletter one of the most widely read in the world... and has helped his readers both avoid catastrophe and make incredible gains.

In addition to *Stansberry's Investment Advisory*, Porter also produces an international-focused investing letter called *Stansberry International*, a bond service called *Stansberry's Credit Opportunities*, and a trading service called *Stansberry Alpha*.

In the following essays, Porter addresses the economic and monetary crisis facing us in America today. He identifies the key to avoiding costly losses during big market panics... the most important steps you can take to not only survive but actually profit from the greatest legal transfer of wealth in history... and how to dramatically – and legally – reduce your U.S. taxes without leaving the country.

How to Prevent Costly Losses During Big Market Panics

It's something no one ever wants to talk about: The horrible, out-of-control feeling that overwhelms investors and leads them to make irrational financial decisions with terrible consequences.

Panic.

For wise investors, it's not a question of *if* other folks are going to panic. It's a question of *when*.

To help you understand what causes investors to panic, let me start with something I doubt you've thought about before: *There are two kinds of panic that affect investors.*

You're probably familiar with the first kind. You might have even felt it. This kind of panic sets in when stocks fall sharply on huge volume.

Now remember the big moves in August 2015. The S&P 500 fell 5% in two days. Then, in early January 2016, the S&P 500 lost another 5%. By February 2016, the market was down 9% since its May 2015 peak.

An important secret lies beneath these moves. *Once you understand this better, you'll never succumb to these feelings again.*

Most people believe that the panic we saw in the market in August 2015 and January 2016 (huge volume, big moves down in stock prices) was the result of emotions. Most people called it a "panicked" selloff. I don't believe it.

Selloffs like that aren't *caused* by emotional behavior. Yes, of course, some people are panicked. Yes, some of those folks are selling. But the huge volume and the big price changes we've seen only happen when lots of investors realize they've made a *big* mistake.

As the realization dawns on them, their reaction is that kind of *determined* selling... no matter what the price. This reflects an important change in the market's basic understanding of the underlying fundamentals.

Something "broke." One (or more) of the major "pegs" of this bull market that had been in place since it started was revealed to be false. And the response by the market participants was urgent and emphatic. This wasn't merely emotional selling. *This was the realization that huge amounts of capital had been misallocated.*

This kind of emphatic selling is the natural result of a lot of bad decisions made in the months and years before the actual panic.

The biggest excesses in the most recent credit bubble were in oil and gas exploration, subprime auto finance, and student loans. That's why you saw such big moves down in General Motors (-17%) and Santander Consumer Finance (-58%). And that's why in the model portfolio of my newsletter *Stansberry's Investment Advisory*, we were stopped out (with some losses and some gains) of most of our remaining oil-related investments (Targa, Union Pacific, Chicago Bridge & Iron, and Nordic American Tankers).

The key to avoiding costly losses during big market panics is to simply avoid making mistakes along the way.

I've been warning about the coming correction in the oil industry and the reckless lending that was propelling the boom since 2012. I've been warning about the coming train wreck in subprime auto lending since 2014. Just a week *before* this market correction, I told my readers exactly why it was inevitable and that it would happen soon. So we weren't surprised. And our portfolio didn't suffer much.

We weren't able to avoid *all* the losses the market endured since last May's high. We don't have a crystal ball. But the *average* gain from the four energy-related companies we were forced to sell was 5.3%.

We avoided taking any big losses because we didn't make many mistakes earlier. *We took profits along the way. We were diversified. And we only bought shares when they were available at good prices.* As a result, we only lost one stock to a trailing stop that wasn't oil-related (glassmaker Corning).

When other investors "panicked," we didn't have to do much of anything because we had made good decisions in the years and months prior to the correction.

Now ask yourself – and be honest...

- Were you diversified enough going into this correction?

- Did you buy "boring" insurance stocks?

- Did you begin to raise some cash?

- Did you buy any precious-metals stocks to hedge your portfolio?

- Did you hold off on buying new investments and wait for this correction?

If you did these things – even just a few of them – the correction wasn't something to be feared at all. *It was something to be celebrated.*

On those panic days in August 2015 and January 2016, capital fled from the weak and the foolish and returned to the wise and the patient. The media, which caters to the lowest common denominator in our society, calls this a "crisis." We call it a victory.

These "panics" are one of the main reasons capitalism works. The virtuous are rewarded. The foolish and greedy are "taxed."

Now... let's talk about the second kind of panic, the kind that few people ever discuss. This is the kind of panic that freezes investors. It leaves them unable to make decisions – often with horrible consequences.

This type of panic is poorly understood. It's almost *never* written about. But it's far more dangerous to you than the first kind of investor panic. There's a secret to understanding this type of fear, too. Once you know where it comes from, it won't ever bother you again.

I've received hundreds of letters that all say the same thing: "*Porter, after the bear market of 2002... or after the financial crisis of 2008... or after the correction of 2011... I was too afraid to buy stocks. I was just frozen. I couldn't pull the trigger...*"

I don't think this correction is finished. The real carnage hasn't even begun. This bull market was built on a few key narratives...

1.   China's growth would propel resource prices forever.

2.   Europe was fixed and would begin to rebound.

3.   The U.S. economic rebound would create a huge new wave of consumer demand.

These things haven't come to pass, and the market is beginning to realize it.

The big problem, which will take a long time to fix, is credit. Credit default swaps have begun to soar in price (revealing credit distress) in big, important businesses. Automakers General Motors and Ford, energy producer Chesapeake Energy, and resource giant Freeport-McMoRan, for example, have all seen big spikes in the cost of credit protection associated with their bonds.

Credit default swaps are how banks, insurance companies, and major hedge funds protect themselves from credit losses. These moves are indicative of a much tougher credit environment moving forward.

These facts are going to scare a lot of investors. Some of them will panic. They will sell everything. They will go to cash. They will miss once-in-a-decade opportunities to buy high-quality businesses – the kind of investments that can multiply your capital by 10 or 50 times in a decade.

That's why I see the idea that the market is probably going lower as *good news.*

I'm building a big list of securities that I'd like to buy. I know I can't time the bottom. All I can hope to do is to buy some world-class businesses at fair prices. I will only have these opportunities if other investors "panic" and refuse to buy stocks because they're afraid of what went wrong during the last cycle.

Here's my theory about panics....

The first kind of panic – like we saw last year – is caused when investors "wise up" and realized they've made some big mistakes.

The second kind of panic – when investors "freeze" and refuse to invest – happens because of ignorance.

It's the second kind that's more likely to prevent you from achieving your financial goals.

Don't panic. Just invest wisely.

We're Approaching a Period of Vast Credit Default

I believe we're facing a huge downturn in the markets. If you're prepared, it will be a great investment period for you – one of the three or four best opportunities in the last 50 years.

If you're not prepared, you'll likely get wiped out.

Credit-market troubles are different than equity-market troubles. Credit-market troubles are "contagious" and are amplified by leverage. Companies funded with equity go bankrupt and nobody notices. But when companies (or countries) funded with huge amounts of debt go bankrupt, it triggers a chain reaction. Institutions that would otherwise be sound can end up in default because they've invested in toxic debt.

That's what's about to happen all around the world.

Far, far, far too much money – mind-boggling amounts – has been borrowed by people and countries that are not creditworthy. These debts are going bad. The chain reaction is starting. And nobody knows exactly what will happen next because the world has never seen so much bad debt before.

This will be the greatest legal transfer of wealth in history.

Students have borrowed more than $1.3 trillion for college. Most of these loans were used to purchase vastly overpriced "online" education of highly dubious value. Consider that in 2000 – just 16 years ago – the largest debt-funded college in the U.S. was New York

University, a highly credible, long-standing institution that serves smart and ambitious students. At the time, former and current NYU students had $2.2 billion in student loans outstanding.

Today, the leading debt-funded college in the U.S. is the University of Phoenix, where $36 billion (yes, that number is real) has been lent to current and former students, almost all of whom received an online education.

Eight of the 10 largest debt-funded universities are online schools. I'd estimate the debts used to fund these educations make up around 80% of all outstanding student loans. *These debts will never be repaid.* And the default tidal wave is starting right now.

Obama issued new rules in 2010 that essentially gave students an option to not repay these debts. Millions have chosen not to. (Shocker!)

These defaults are now spilling over into securitized-debt packages worth hundreds of millions of dollars. They, too, will default, damaging our financial system in ways no one yet understands.

Elsewhere, big emerging markets with fragile, corrupt governments (Mexico, Brazil, Turkey, and Greece) have borrowed mind-boggling sums of money denominated largely in U.S. dollars. These loans will all go bad.

Brazil's currency has already fallen by more than 40% over the past two years. That's tantamount to its loan balances growing by 40% because so much of its debt is denominated in U.S. dollars. The trouble is even worse in smaller markets, like Malaysia and Indonesia, whose currencies are trading at 17-year lows.

When you read about other countries' currencies falling apart, you should know it will eventually harm our own banking system and bond markets, which have financed all the debts...

Over the last decade, the emerging-markets bond market has grown faster than any other debt market – by more than 600%. In only 10 years, emerging-markets debts have gone from about 20% the size of the U.S. high-yield market to roughly equal the U.S. high-yield market. That means a much, much higher percentage of the world's fixed-income securities have significant currency and political risk than ever before.

Nearly all the growth in the U.S. high-yield bond market over the last decade is related to oil and gas exploration and production.

Since 2010, more than $300 billion of new corporate debt was raised for U.S. onshore oil and gas producers. It's this capital that financed the oil boom – which is responsible for all the net job creation in the U.S. since 2009.

These debts cannot be repaid with oil prices at less than $60 a barrel, much less $30 (as they are in March 2016). And yet they're all coming due between 2016 and 2020.

As these debts go bad, even major oil companies will see their bonds downgraded and their dividends cut. There will be a huge opportunity for patient and liquid investors to buy tremendous energy assets out of these defaults. But for the banks, insurance companies, private-equity funds, and pension funds that provided this initial capital, there's a tremendous amount of pain ahead. Expect major bank collapses in Texas.

The auto-buying boom of 2010-2014 was financed with extraordinarily dubious subprime loans. As recently as December 2015, 60% of General Motors' loan book in North America was subprime, with a shocking amount categorized as "deep subprime." Deep subprime is essentially people who don't have a credit rating or people who are currently in bankruptcy.

These loans were made using new, much-longer terms – 72 and 84 months. Given the high interest rates on subprime car loans (around 20%), these car "buyers" won't own any equity – zero – in the cars until after month 60. For five years, they have no economic interest in the vehicle they "own."

These loans are the auto equivalent of a subprime home buyer who used his mortgage as a piggy bank between 2004 and 2007.

By the end of September 2015, total auto loans outstanding in the U.S. had reached more than $1 trillion – up nearly 25% in only two years. Does that sound wise? Loans that originated in 2014 have begun to default at a pace not seen since the 2008 financial crisis.

This problem is going to get a lot worse. It will probably result in bankruptcy at Ford Motor and massive losses to financial institutions that own these auto loans, like GM Financial and Santander Consumer USA.

Even investors who aren't directly hit by any of these ticking debt time bombs are going to be severely hurt by the coming wave of debt defaults. That's because corporate America can rarely resist taking a good idea (buying back stock) and making it into a farce.

It should seem obvious to everyone that buying back stock when it's cheap (like in 2009) is a great use of a corporation's free cash flow (earnings in excess of capital investments).

It should also be apparent to all investors that borrowing huge sums of money to buy back stock *after* a six-year raging bull market will likely cause severe financial problems sooner or later. That's especially true when the company in question is *already* highly leveraged and when it operates in highly cyclical industries or industries whose earnings are largely dictated by borrowing costs (like real estate).

The following table shows five companies whose debt-funded buybacks over the past year go so far beyond merely "stupid" that their actions cry out for an investigation of the management team (and a complete replacement of their boards).

LEADERS IN VALUE DESTRUCTION

Name	Excess Buybacks*	Debt to Equity**	Debt to Cash Earnings***
American Airlines (AAL)	4,208%	368%	212
McGraw Hill (MHFI)	2,111%	310%	64
Deere & Co (DE)	698%	545%	86
Enterprise Products Partners (EPD)	440%	108%	55
Simon Property Group (SPG)	402%	429%	38

* Percentage of free cash flow (FCF) used to purchase stock or pay dividends over the last four quarters
** Current debt-to-equity ratio
*** Total debt to FCF over the last four quarters (Years to pay off debt with FCF)

www.stansberryresearch.com

The people running these companies are driving into a brick wall... and pressing harder on the accelerator.

How will you know if this dark view of the world is correct? Just keep your eye on the exchange-traded funds (ETFs) that hold vast quantities of speculative debt.

For example, I track the iShares iBoxx High Yield Corporate Bond Fund (HYG) every day. I've been warning you about it since May 2013. Since then, it has fallen from $95 to less than $80... It made a new low in early 2016.

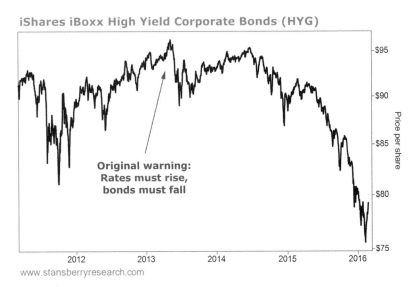

iShares iBoxx High Yield Corporate Bonds (HYG)

Original warning:
Rates must rise,
bonds must fall

www.stansberryresearch.com

As long as this downtrend remains in place, you can know for certain that I'm 100% right.

Here's My Promise About All This

First, we're about to see a lot of big, wealthy investors panic when they realize how much of this garbage they own.

Anyone who is currently invested across the fixed-income markets will end up taking losses on the bad debt I just described because it makes up such a large percentage of the total fixed-income universe.

Remember: Fannie Mae and Freddie Mac told investors they didn't own any subprime debt. It was a total lie. They held hundreds of billions of dollars of worthless mortgages. That will happen again with the bad debt.

When you hear a major financial institution claim it doesn't own any emerging market debt or any subprime auto or student loans... don't believe it.

Second, unless you follow our work, you will likely suffer the second kind of panic. You'll likely freeze up. You'll be too scared to buy anything.

I met a smart and talented financial analyst at a December 2008 meeting in Hong Kong, right in the middle of the crisis. He had been looking at parking garages in central Hong Kong – some of the most valuable real estate in the world. The yields on the properties were more than 20%. But he wouldn't buy. He admitted that he was too scared things would get even worse and no one would be able to afford to park their cars.

Don't make that kind of mistake.

The world isn't coming to an end. All that's going to change is that these assets are going to shift from the leveraged and foolish to the wise and patient.

The coming crisis will be terrible for most investors. But it can be GREAT for you.

One of the most important steps you can take to protect yourself is to hold a large position in cash and gold...

How to Raise Cash, Safeguard It, and Hedge It With Gold

During a bear market, nothing is more important than cash.

It's not hard to understand the basics of why cash is so important. In fact, you could define a bear market as the rising value of the U.S. dollar versus financial assets.

Likewise, when commodities... or real estate... or foreign currencies... go through a bear market, what you're really seeing is the rising value of the U.S. dollar as compared with those other assets.

As you can see in the following chart, while the price of just about everything else has been falling, the U.S. dollar is on the rise...

In Bear Markets, the Dollar Rallies

www.stansberryresearch.com

17

Therefore, the most important factor in determining how successful you can be as an investor during a bear market is simply how much cash you have (and can raise) as asset prices fall.

Or as the legendary editor of *The Dow Theory Letters* Richard Russell taught me, the key to winning in a bear market is to simply not lose anything.

Russell wrote about the stock market for seven decades, from the late 1940s until just before he died in November 2015 at the age of 91. He was a mentor of mine. I've carefully studied the lessons he taught about bear markets.

Russell's Primary Trend Index (the famous "PTI") turned bearish in late-August 2015, after the market fell 1,000 points in a day. This big change in the market's momentum, along with the poor performance of the Dow Jones Transportation Index, once again provided a warning of an impending bear market.

In our daily *Digest* newsletter, we offered a different kind of warning – just before this big market move.

On August 14, 2015, we wrote that a bear market was inevitable because the economic gains made in America between 2009 and 2015 were all part of a "phony" credit boom engineered by our central bank…

> The [Federal Reserve] has provided $4 trillion in additional credit to the U.S. Treasury. Saving didn't create this credit. It was created out of thin air…
>
> For the last six years, this immense amount of credit has artificially reduced the cost of capital across our entire economy – lowering it to almost zero. It's as though the Fed suspended "gravity" in our economy. And not surprisingly, a boom erupted where this credit landed…
>
> In the short term, these policies have stimulated our economy. Texas led employment growth following the last

recession. Outside of employment related to oil investments, employment hasn't grown at all in the U.S.

Likewise, the two other booming areas of our economy have been auto sales (which neared an all-time high last year with 17 million new cars sold) and capital investment in higher education. Drive through any major university, and you will see plenty of cranes.

The only forms of consumer credit that have grown since 2009 are student loans and car loans. Total outstanding car loans passed $1 trillion for the first time ever. But where will this lead us?

The credit stimulation our economy received was phony. The capital wasn't earned or saved. The positive result was a boom. But these investments and this consumer borrowing happened in an environment nearly free of capital costs (zero gravity). In this world, almost anything would "fly."

A lot of the money invested in the oil business, for example, has gone into projects (like the oil sands) that aren't economic and aren't likely to be in a lifetime. A lot of cars were built and sold to people who can't actually afford them. These people will eventually default. Sooner or later, soaring car-loan defaults will drive down the prices of used cars, making it difficult to sell new ones at a profit.

That's the downside to a phony boom. Since these investments weren't financed with actual savings, there won't be enough demand to sustain the debts that have been created.

You can think of savings and investments as a see-saw. Without roughly the same amounts on either side, you're going to have a problem.

For the last six years, that has meant our economy was on "tilt" in a way most people think of as positive: Huge

> investments in oil and plenty of credit for consumers. Now, the opposite kind of "tilt" looms right in front of us. The boom, as it was not financed with savings, will surely lead to a bust of similar magnitude. – Porter Stansberry on Economic Gravity, the Stansberry Digest, August 14, 2015

Based on these fundamental and technical factors, we began to add "short" positions in the model portfolio of our flagship newsletter, *Stansberry's Investment Advisory*. We continued to issue warning after warning about the economic "lions" devouring investors' portfolios: emerging markets, commodity prices, corporate bonds, and transportation stocks.

Then, in early 2016, the bear-market trends intensified, making it impossible for most investors to ignore the risks of a major bear market.

And so... we return to Richard Russell's wisdom.

The goal of investors during a bear market is, first and foremost, not to lose anything. But in a complex world of paper currencies and constant devaluations engineered by central banks... where is there any permanent value? What's the safest form of cash available today?

Unless you have a substantial amount of cash, it will be difficult (or impossible) for you to act on the other strategies you will want to pursue during a bear market.

Therefore, the most important thing you have to do to survive a bear market is to raise a substantial amount of cash.

We recommend holding at least 40% of your investment assets in cash. And to protect the purchasing power of these savings, *we also recommend holding at least 10% of your portfolio in gold.* We believe gold is absolutely critical. It's the only way to protect yourself from the near-certain actions of central bankers, who will try to devalue the dollar as a means of easing the ongoing debt liquidation.

As you'll see, gold is the other side of the "coin" in our cash strategy.

First, let me take a moment to talk about what "cash" means and why it's critical to have during a bear market (or an economic crisis).

What Is 'Cash'?

Simply put, cash is the most commonly used means of exchange in any economy.

In the United States, cash means the U.S. dollar. The dollar is a "fiat" currency. That means it is not backed by any firm value. It's not exchangeable for gold or any other reserve asset. It's money only because the government says so – legal tender. It's the kind of money that you must use to pay your taxes and your debts.

We could have a long philosophical debate about whether or not the dollar should be money in the U.S. (or anywhere else). But this is a practical guide to tactical asset allocation. So when we talk about "going to cash," "raising cash," or making sure that your portfolio holds plenty of cash... we're talking about the U.S. dollar.

We recognize that the dollar (and every other fiat currency) is deeply flawed and inherently unstable. It's entirely possible that the current debt debacle is the beginning of the dollar's demise. But even so, you need to hold plenty of dollars during a bear market. Why? Because **by definition, a bear market is the rising value of the dollar relative to financial assets**.

Again, let us stress that we're fully aware of the serious risks all dollar-holders face. That's why we're going to not only show you how to hold cash safely, but more important, how to "hedge" your dollar exposure through a wide range of gold investments.

Most investors (including legendary investor Warren Buffett) simply don't understand gold or its real purpose in your portfolio. So let's address that right now.

Why Gold?

Gold is not an investment. (Buying gold stocks, on the other hand, is an investment.)

Throughout history, gold has been the most secure, least volatile, most international, and least political form of money. It continues to offer us the same utility today. Gold is a perfect currency because...

It's rare: All the gold that has ever been mined could fit under the Eiffel Tower.

It's not consumed: Gold has zero large-scale industrial uses. Virtually all the gold ever mined still exists in the form of bullion, bars, coins, and jewelry.

It's unchanging: Gold never tarnishes. You could bury a bar in your backyard today, and it would still shine 100 years from now. (We don't recommend doing this, by the way.) Even gold coins left on the seafloor for hundreds of years can be cleaned to a brilliant shine.

It's universally accepted and acknowledged: Every major culture in the world reveres gold and uses it as a private form of money and savings.

It isn't anyone else's liability: Even in a world of collapsing credit standards, failing banks, and bankrupt bonds, gold never defaults. It's nature's triple-A-asset.

It's portable: Sure, diamonds might be more portable... but putting $20 million worth of rare coins in a suitcase isn't difficult. In a crisis, having a few million dollars in gold is going to be a lot easier to handle than trying to manage the same value in silver.

It holds its value: This is gold's most important feature, and the one that's the least understood. Gold is a kind of financial scale. Its value never changes. Sure, the price of gold might change, but its value won't. Price is a ratio, in this case comparing gold with dollars. So when the price of gold changes, what's really happening is that the value of the dollar is changing.

The amount of gold in existence increases by less than 1% a year. People talk about trading gold – that's just nuts. Gold will remain the same. It's the other assets that are moving around gold.

As I said, gold is the scale. Its value is the closest thing we have to permanent in this world. And that's the No. 1 reason you want to own gold during a crisis. Whether you're worried about inflation or a deflationary debt collapse... gold will remain unchanged in value.

Just remember: Gold is the scale. Its value won't change.

I've been working for investors for 20 years... and one of my favorite things to do is to introduce people to gold. If you've never seen gold coins up close or never held a few in your hand, do yourself a favor. Go to a gold coin show. Or call up a local dealer. Go buy a coin or two. Hold them in your hand.

Trust me, if feels great. That's "real money" you're holding, not the paper junk we use today.

When you're holding gold in your hand, you'll understand immediately why human beings have revered gold for all of history, and you'll see how debauched our fiat currency has become... the difference in quality between a beautiful Saint-Gaudens $20 gold piece and the garbage we carry in our pockets today.

All right... that's enough about the definitions. You now know what we're talking about when we recommend holding at least 40% of your portfolio in cash and at least 10% in gold. But... how can you do that safely?

How to Raise Cash and How to Hold It

Believe it or not... not everything in finance and investing has to be complicated.

For most readers, raising cash will be as easy as deciding which investments you want to sell. (An easy way to decide is to simply follow your exit strategies, like trailing stop losses.) As you sell securities, your cash balance in your brokerage account will grow.

Make sure you understand how this cash balance is being managed. Call your broker and ask if your cash balance is being "swept" overnight into a money-market fund. If it is, request that your broker not do this, even if that means you suffer a reduction in interest income.

In the midst of a credit-default cycle, you don't want to own any kind of fixed-income mutual, money-market, or exchange-traded funds (ETFs). You simply can't know what they're actually holding.

Most people will not exceed the $250,000 Securities Investor Protection Corp. (SIPC) protection limits for cash in a brokerage account or the $250,000 limit for Federal Deposit Insurance Corp. (FDIC) bank accounts. For these people, going to cash is easy. They just need to sell securities until they reach a 40% cash allocation (or more – sell down until you can sleep well at night).

If your cash balance exceeds the SIPC or FDIC limits, we recommend you buy U.S. Treasury bills as your cash-holding vehicle. You can buy 30-, 60-, or 90-day bills. All are acceptable in terms of meeting our definition of a "cash" portion of your portfolio. Investors can buy directly from the Treasury online. Just use this website: http://www.treasurydirect.gov/tdhome.htm.

If you don't want to deal with the hassle of buying Treasury bills directly for whatever reason, the next best alternative is the **SPDR Barclays 1-3 Month T-Bill Fund (NYSE: BIL)**. This is the only short-term U.S. Treasury bill pure play. The problem is, despite the fund's low annual fees (0.14%), the interest rates are so low on these forms of government debt that you could suffer a small annual loss (less than 1%) because of the fees.

So if you're dealing with a substantial amount of cash (more than $100,000), please take the time to set up an account with Treasury Direct.

The other alternative is to call your broker's government-bond desk and buy short-term zero-coupon bonds. Zero-coupon bonds are a financial asset you buy at a discount from their face value (or "par"), allowing capital gains to accrue rather than receiving a coupon payment. Typically, these bonds are available in durations from three to 12 months and in denominations of $1,000 to $5,000.

Let's say you wanted to safeguard $10,000. You would call your broker and tell him to buy U.S. Treasury zero-coupon bonds for any of these durations:

- $9,994.60 for the three-month bond.

- $9,984.70 for the six-month bond.

- $9,968.40 for the 12-month bond.

At maturity, you'd receive $10,000.

As you can see, you earn virtually nothing in these bonds. That's the downside of holding cash. The upside is, at least you'll get your principal back. Remember: The goal during a bear market is not to lose money. If you can just avoid losing money, you'll do fine because the bear market will create lots of opportunities to make big gains going forward.

That's it.

Learning how to manage your cash isn't hard. Gold, on the other hand, is a different story.

How to Own Gold

There are four basic forms of gold you should own.

The first form is simple bullion. Bullion coins are plain, vanilla, gold coins. They're not rare and they don't have collectible value. You can buy them and sell them for a few dollars more than the spot price of gold.

Most gold coins come in one-ounce increments. The premium dealers charge for bullion gold over the market – or "spot" – price varies depending on supply and demand. The price of gold is currently around $1,225 per ounce. One-ounce bullion coins currently go for around $35-$55 more than spot gold. For example, in early 2016, an American Eagle or American Buffalo trades for around $1,275. A South African Krugerrand trades for around $1,325.

You can also buy bars, if you've got deep pockets. It's fun to keep a bar of gold on your coffee table.

"What's that?"

"Oh, that... it's a bar of gold. Try to pick it up."

Gold bars come in one-, 10-, and 400-ounce denominations. Usually, bars are the cheapest way to buy physical gold bullion. You will pay about $35 more than the spot price for a one-ounce bar and $5 more than spot for a 400-ounce bar. In general, the bigger the bar you purchase, the cheaper the gold per ounce.

You can buy bullion coins from any local coin dealer. We recommend calling several shops to find the one charging the lowest markup over spot.

There are also online services that enable you to buy bullion and hold it in a secured physical vault.

One way to invest in gold is through BullionVault. At BullionVault, you can buy gold and have it held in "good delivery" form. BullionVault charges a commission rate of 0.5%, which falls progressively to 0.05% the more you buy. Discounts start at $75,000.

There are also currency transfer fees, plus storage and insurance expenses to consider, which will depend on your purchase amount and requirements. To get started, go to www.bullionvault.com and click "Open Account" located in the top right-hand corner.

The second form of gold we recommend is rare or collectible coins. These coins – known in the industry as "semi-numismatic" coins – are old. They're gorgeous. And they have collectible value. In good condition, they sell for thousands of dollars more than the spot price of gold.

One of the most famous collectible coins – and the best one to purchase – is the $20 Saint-Gaudens. The proper name for this coin is a $20 Double Eagle gold coin. But coin experts call them "$20 Saints" because legendary American sculptor Augustus Saint-Gaudens designed them.

To give you some history, people in the late 19th century used gold coins as currency. They bought steamboat tickets with them. They purchased houses with them. They even paid bills with them. The vast majority of the gold coins from this era that exist today are in "junk" condition. They're worn down and scratched up, like most of the coins in your pocket. Few "uncirculated" gold coins exist from this era.

In the early 20th century, America became the largest economy on Earth. As a result, America's $20 gold piece became the world's most important coin. The U.S. Mint produced 70 million $20 gold coins between 1907 and 1933.

Paper money eventually took over as currency for day-to-day transactions, and gold coins became a savings instrument. Savers kept these coins in sock drawers, safety deposit boxes, and bank vaults. Hundreds of thousands of uncirculated gold coins are still in existence from this era.

Coins are categorized by year, type, and grade. The grade rates the coin's condition on a scale of one (lowest) to 70 (highest). Most coins you will find in a coin shop will range from AU-55 ("almost" or "about uncirculated") to MS-67 ("mint state" or "not circulated"). Obviously, the higher the quality, the more you pay for a coin.

Truly uncirculated, pristine $20 Saints are so beautiful and rare that collectors pay tens of thousands of dollars for them. That's not the kind of coin we're focusing on here.

With low-premium semi-numismatic coins, you are looking for the AU-58 to MS-62 range. This will give you historic coins in beautiful condition with the lowest premium for numismatic value.

Right now, you can purchase them for about $1,400 to $1,500. That's $200-$300 more than a bullion coin. For the additional money, you get some historical value – which is unlikely to go much lower.

Specifically, look for $20 Double Eagles in the MS-60 to MS-62 range. They have more upside potential than any other gold bullion investment. For the last 40 years, these coins have commanded a significant premium over gold bullion coins. During the 1960s, when gold was trading at $32 per ounce, these $20 Saints sold for almost $65 per coin... a 100% premium over gold. In 2001, when gold was trading at $300 an ounce, these $20 Saints traded for $710-$750 each... as much as a 150% premium.

Right now, you can buy a pre-1933 Saint-Gaudens in that grade for $200-$300 more than a Krugerrand or an Eagle. The premiums are close to all-time lows at about 18%-30%.

To get started, we encourage you to look over the excellent price guide put out by Professional Coin Grading Service (PCGS). The values listed on its website are good estimates of what you should expect to pay.

Please remember, with collectible coins, it's crucial to go to a reliable and trusted coin broker. It's extremely rare to buy a fake. The bigger problem is paying for a grade higher than what the coin truly is. Paying a little extra in premium to a trusted coin dealer is worth it. This way, when you're buying an MS-62 coin, you can be confident that it's really that grade and not lower.

There are many reputable dealers. One we know well and who has treated our subscribers well in the past is David Hall Rare Coins. To get the latest quotes – and the latest expert advice on where to find the greatest values in gold and silver coins – contact David Hall or his business partner Van Simmons at (800) 759-7575 or (949) 567-1325 or via e-mail at info@davidhall.com.

Finally, look for coins graded by reputable services. Collectors and dealers send their coins to grading services to have them assigned grades. The services have experts who grade and put the coins in a case. But not all grading services are the same.

PCGS is the most respected and reliable grading service. Numismatic Guaranty Corp. (NGC) is the probably the second-most respected. If you ever want to sell your numismatic coins back to a dealer, they usually pay a premium for ones graded by PCGS.

The third form of gold we recommend is the Central Fund of Canada (NYSE: CEF).

The Central Fund of Canada – which bills itself as the "Sound Monetary Fund" – is an Alberta, Canada-based investment company that passively holds gold and silver bullion. It doesn't buy, sell, or trade its precious metals in an attempt to improve returns. It doesn't deal in futures contracts for the metals. All it does is sit on a big vault of gold and silver. Buying a share of CEF simply gives you a small ownership stake in the metals it owns.

My friend and colleague Steve Sjuggerud has written extensively about CEF. He shares his work on investing in CEF in Part 5 of this book.

The fourth form of gold we recommend is gold stocks. Be careful with gold stocks. Gold mining is a terrible business and very, very few gold-mining stocks do well for investors. But we recommend some exposure to the highest-quality gold-mining assets because it's a cheap way to own a lot of gold (in the ground), and these businesses can turn out to be incredibly good investments – especially when stocks in general do poorly.

Think of your gold stocks as "lottery tickets" that will probably be worthless in 10 years... but just might end up making you 10 or 20 times your money. (If that happens, don't forget to sell!)

Build an 'Escape Hatch' and Cut Your Taxes Without Leaving America

This might be the greatest tax loophole in America...

It's a way to essentially remove yourself from onerous U.S. tax liability without leaving the U.S. and without giving up your citizenship.

By using this rarely publicized loophole, you can reduce your federal income tax burden by up to 90% – and eliminate your taxes at the state level entirely.

But if it's this good... and true... why isn't everyone doing it?

This loophole won't make sense for everyone. But it is something every American should consider at some point.

Think of it as an escape hatch...

A friend of Stansberry Research personally used this "hatch." He proudly announced he had packed up and left California for the Caribbean.

But he didn't give up his citizenship or break any laws. And he lowered his company's tax bill by 90%.

In this chapter, we highlight exactly how you, too, can save tens of thousands of dollars each year... money that you used to pay to the U.S. government.

What Makes the U.S. Virgin Islands Special

Before we begin, please note that this strategy is not for everyone. You need to be willing to relocate (at least for part of the year) to the U.S. Virgin Islands. And you have to bring a real operating business along with you... one that you can credibly claim creates local jobs.

If that describes you, we urge you to seek out a good local tax attorney who can determine how your business – and its owners – can take advantage of significant tax incentives.

The key to this strategy lies within the resort-lined beaches of the U.S. Virgin Islands...

The U.S. acquired its portion of the Virgin Islands in 1917. It bought them from Denmark by signing the Treaty of the Danish West Indies one year earlier.

The major livable islands that make up the U.S. Virgin Islands are St. Thomas, St. John, and St. Croix. These three islands sit about 100 miles east of Puerto Rico. The eastern tip of St. Croix is called Point Udall, the easternmost piece of U.S. territory.

The Virgin Islands are a territory of the U.S., which means getting there is easy... You don't need a passport to enter. There's no complicated customs procedure. And you don't need to change money.

It's just like flying to Key West, Florida, or Maui, Hawaii, or any other domestic destination that has a commercial runway adjacent to a picturesque, turquoise ocean.

The U.S. Virgin Islands are one of 16 U.S. territories. Others you've probably heard of include Puerto Rico, Guam, and American Samoa. Initially, the U.S. acquired each of these for strategic reasons. As time passed, the U.S. realized these remote territories could become a drain on domestic resources.

So as a part of the Naval Appropriations Act for 1922, the U.S. ordered residents of the U.S. Virgin Islands to pay income taxes directly to the territory's taxing authority... instead of the newly organized Internal Revenue Service (IRS).

As a result, residents of the Virgin Island are U.S. citizens with U.S. passports... but they don't have to file a tax return with the IRS.

Instead, each of the U.S. territories is required to use what's called a "mirror code." That means each of these independent taxing authorities has to use the U.S. tax code when assessing and collecting taxes from territory residents.

But there's an important loophole... one that most people miss entirely. The U.S. granted each territory the right to create economic incentives to promote growth through Section 934 of the U.S. tax code. From the IRS...

> § 934(b)(1) grants limited authority to the USVI to reduce the USVI tax liability with respect to income from USVI sources or income effectively connected with a trade or business within the USVI.

The U.S. Virgin Islands Economic Development Authority sets the territory's incentives through its Economic Development Commission (EDC) program. There's also a program through the University of the Virgin Islands ("UVI") and Technology Park ("RTPark").

There's no one-size-fits-all plan. And as we said, you need to be a resident of the U.S. Virgin Islands... and you need to have a real business. But there are many ways to qualify for EDC tax-related benefits. A good tax attorney can help minimize your tax bill.

A broad range of industries currently receive EDC or UVI RTPark tax benefits... from manufacturing and assembly companies, hotels, and high-tech companies. Here are a few real examples of people and companies who have legally reduced their income taxes by 90%...

A Few Folks Who Have Slashed Their Tax Bills

The friend of Stansberry Research we mentioned earlier is the chief operating officer of a small gold-mine finance company. The company is similar to Silver Wheaton (SLW). His company is private and is funded by a group of U.S. investors who asked us not to directly mention their names.

The company's owners spend half the year in South Florida and the other half in St. Thomas. The company finances gold projects on five continents and can conduct its business from anywhere in the world.

This is exactly the type of business the U.S. Virgin Islands is looking for. The company's management team moved its operations to the island... bringing demand for other services with it.

This year, the company will save several million dollars on its reduced tax bill compared with the 35% rate it would pay if it were instead headquartered in the continental U.S. More important, the owners also benefit from a 90% reduction in their personal income tax bill, meaning those profits are not "double taxed" the way corporate earnings are in the U.S.

In the case of publicly traded Ocwen Financial (OCN), a $340 million market cap mortgage loan servicer, the numbers are even larger. The company made headlines last year for having difficulty with state regulators supervising its subprime-loan-servicing business. But it hasn't had any trouble with its tax bill since relocating to St. Croix in 2013. According to *Newsweek* magazine, the move lowered the company's effective tax rate to 11.9% from 30% a year earlier. The magazine went on to state...

> While plenty of non-U.S. havens have come under intense media attention in recent years, there is little focus on the U.S. Virgin Islands, the only nearly tax-free haven in the world to fly the American flag.

The *average* rate of corporate taxes paid in the U.S. Virgin Islands is just 3.4%, according to the same *Newsweek* analysis.

Or take U.S. Viking, a technology company featured on the USVI Economic Development Authority website... Its primary product is ENPS, a newsroom computer system marketed by the Associated

Press. More than 800 newsrooms – including ESPN and the BBC – use its products. And U.S. Viking pays far, far lower taxes than if it were headquartered anywhere else in the U.S.

Of course, folks in the U.S. Virgin Islands are tight-lipped about how much in taxes they pay. They don't want the secret getting out...

'This Is the Place for People Who Hate Taxes'

The U.S. Virgin Islands is the ideal place for people who want to legally reduce their tax bill. The territory's former governor, John de Jongh, tours the U.S. to advertise the benefits of relocating to the islands. As he said in an *International Business Times* article...

> Our program is sanctioned by the Congress and the U.S. Treasury... It's a safe environment for [businesses] to operate.

De Jongh goes on to point out that this arrangement is perfectly legal and avoids the perils of illegal tax dodging. Relocating to the U.S. Virgin Islands means that in addition to tremendous savings on your tax bill, you and your money can travel freely. But there are other benefits to establishing residency in the U.S. Virgin Islands...

If your child is born in a U.S. territory, he is still automatically a U.S. citizen. But at the end of his life, he's not subject to federal estate taxes if he dies as a resident of the territory.

The same is true for immigrants. If you're not a U.S. citizen and are considering becoming one, you might consider doing so in a U.S. territory. The citizenship is just as good as the one you'd get in any of the 50 U.S. states, but when you die, your heirs will benefit from 100% of your hard-earned assets instead of 50% after estate taxes are levied.

And that's what's great about the U.S. Virgin Islands... You don't have to break the law. You also don't have to smuggle your life savings to some remote outpost to evade taxation. You don't even have to change banks or uproot your entire family.

You do have to spend 183 days each year in the U.S. Virgin Islands... where the temperature rarely falls below 75 degrees or rises above 85 degrees. For that matter... if your spouse misses the cold, only you have to go. The tax code exemptions stipulate only the higher-income earner on a jointly filed return must meet the definition of a bona fide resident.

You also have to run a real business, one that creates employment for locals. So this program is not for everyone. But if you qualify, the benefits are massive. The *New York Times* summarized the program this way...

> The [EDC] offers companies a number of inducements, including a 90 percent exemption on local income taxes; a 90 percent exemption on dividends; a 100 percent exemption on gross receipts taxes; a 100 percent exemption on property taxes; a 100 percent exemption on excise taxes; and 1 percent customs duties. The creation of the commission was accompanied by an aggressive marketing campaign, which resulted in about 100 companies moving to or expanding on the islands between 2002 and 2004, employing nearly 3,100 people.
>
> "Of course there's a trade-off," said Nadine Marchena, the commission's assistant chief executive. "In exchange for the benefits, we expect our companies to invest in the community. We ask them to buy locally, support regional charities and establish residency – anything that demonstrates an intention to stay."

So you can't just move to the islands and stop paying taxes.

You have to do a little work first... and the advice of a tax lawyer will be invaluable. You set up a meeting, fly down, explain a little about your current income and business, and he'll let you know how the EDC or UVI RTPark program could lower your taxes. It's that easy.

One of the Only Legal Ways to Avoid Paying the IRS

Everyone wants to pay fewer taxes. But when you try to skirt the law, it always takes a toll on your life. Your hard-earned money is in jeopardy, and so is your freedom.

And there's always the risk that a big chunk of your wealth ends up trapped in some faraway place that later turns into an inhospitable environment. Imagine if you had stashed your life savings in Argentina a decade ago... Today, it would be worth half as much and you wouldn't be able to get it out.

This is why we are only interested in *legal* ways to lower our tax bill. And we're not alone... A lot of smart folks are taking advantage of this loophole.

While it's impossible to get a look at anyone's personal tax returns, it's easy to see who is hanging around the U.S. Virgin Islands. For example...

Notable liberal and high-taxation advocate Paul Krugman has a home on St. Croix and spends a lot of time there. Vice President Joe Biden's brother owns property on Water Island, which is just south of St. Thomas. And U.S. Representative Chellie Pingree got into a lot of trouble because her husband, billionaire hedge-fund investor S. Donald Sussman, claimed to be a resident of both the U.S. Virgin Islands and Maine.

People in-the-know with good legal counsel are already taking advantage of this extraordinary loophole. They know that earning lots of money is good... But if you give half of it back in taxes, you're not getting ahead. Managing your tax liability is just as important as earning income.

The tax advantages of relocating to the U.S. Virgin Islands are numerous and broad. But again, we remind you that it's essential that you consult with a tax expert to determine what you can qualify for.

If you're working for a large U.S. company that requires you to show up at an office every single day, it might be difficult for you to take advantage of this. But if you're a small-business owner who is tired of paying huge amounts of taxes to the IRS, it may be worth looking into.

It's at least worth spending a few days in St. Croix and meeting with an experienced and reputable tax attorney. You could be missing out on the chance to save a tremendous amount of money.

And while we can't guarantee your trip to the tax lawyer will pay off, we *can* guarantee you won't be disappointed by the views...

Porter Stansberry's Top Ideas

- The key to avoiding costly losses during a market panic is to simply avoid making mistakes along the way. Take profits. Diversify. Only buy shares at good prices.

- Hold at least 40% of your investment assets in cash. Do this by buying **Treasury Bills** or **SPDR Barclays 1-3 Month T-Bill Fund (NYSE: BIL)**.

- Protect the purchasing power of your cash by holding at least 10% of your portfolio in gold. You have the option of owning bullion, collectible coins, gold stocks, or buying **Central Fund of Canada (NYSE: CEF)**. Each gold investment has a unique set of pros and cons. Decide what works best for you.

- If you're a small business owner, legally escape paying U.S. taxes by living half the year in the Virgin Islands.

Bill Bonner

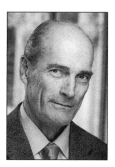

Bill Bonner founded Agora Inc. in 1979. It is now one of the largest independent newsletter publishing companies in the world.

Today, Bill is chairman of Bonner & Partners and editor of *The Bill Bonner Letter* (his monthly newsletter) and *Bill Bonner's Diary* (his daily e-letter). He has co-written the bestselling books *Financial Reckoning Day* and *Empire of Debt*. His independent works include *Mobs, Messiahs and Markets... Dice Have No Memory...* and *Hormegeddon: How Too Much of a Good Thing Leads to Disaster.*

In all his writings, Bill shares insights and ideas about how financial worlds really work. But he isn't a stock-picker. Instead, he identifies big opportunities. He shows his readers where average investors are making mistakes. He details opportunities that he's interested in personally. In short, Bill opens a window to the world that you simply won't find anywhere else.

In the next several pages, Bill details the social and economic problems facing the middle class. He introduces the "investment compass" and answers that all-important question: *What should you do with your money now?*

You might not agree with everything he says. But we guarantee it will teach you a thing or two about the future of wealth-building in America – and your place in it.

Confessions of a One-Percenter

Economist Larry Summers, bless his heart, is arguing for more stimulus, more spending, more central planning for the economy, and more control of our money. We should send him a 'Thank You.'

Yes, dear reader, I confess. I'm a member of the "1%" – the few, the lucky, the rich. Well, I don't know if I really qualify for the top 1%... but thanks to Larry Summers, I must be getting close.

If you believe the press reports, the top 10% are greedy bastards who rigged the world financial system, soured its economy, and ruined millions of decent, hardworking families. But I had nothing to do with rigging the system. Who did? Larry, Alan, Ben, Janet, Mario... along with thousands of other economists, politicians, bureaucrats, and cronies.

Of course, there are benefits to being at the top. And not just the money. We live in better houses. We live longer. Our women aren't as fat, and our men aren't as thick.

Besides, somebody's got to be at the top of the heap. But lately, the distance between the top and the bottom has stretched the socio-economic pyramid into a grotesque new shape, with the rich so far above the poor we can no longer smell their sweat or feel their pain.

Naturally, right-thinking economists call for "reform." Especially those that caused the problem in the first place.

Thanks, again! We all know the reforms they want – redistribution, taxes, and regulation – are those that make the rich richer. Money talks. Politicians have an acute sense of hearing. The "reformers" can hear a dog whistle.

Gina Rinehart, one of the richest women on the planet, can tell the poor that they need to "stop drinking, stop smoking, and work harder." It's not only a convenient myth... it's also a useful one. Earning money the old-fashioned, honest way is still your best bet... unless you've got the government or the central bank in your pocket.

Oops! I've let the cat out of the bag.

In economics, the phenomenon is known as the "Cantillon Effect." Economist and author Richard Cantillon was an associate of John Law, the world's first fully modern central banker. Cantillon noticed that Law's new paper money – backed by shares in the Mississippi Company – didn't reach everyone at the same rate.

The insiders – that is, the rich and the well-connected – got the paper first. They competed for goods and services with it... just as though it was as good as the old money. By the time it reached the laboring classes, however, this new money had been greatly discounted... eventually, to the point where it was worthless.

(Cantillon himself was a beneficiary of this phenomenon. He speculated in Law's Mississippi Company shares. Then, foreseeing disaster, he sold out at the top. This so enraged the buyers, who were ruined, that they plotted to murder him. Cantillon may have staged his own death to escape them.)

A version of the Cantillon Effect was observed in Soviet gulags and German concentration camps. Victims reported that those who were close to the kitchen were more likely to survive. The food often ran out before it reached those who worked in the fields and forests.

Now, we have the central banks running their printing presses – effectively giving money to their friends in the banking industry. From there, it seeps into the whole financial community, boosting prices for financial assets, which are owned by... you guessed it... the 10%.

Speculators and investors make money. English economist John Maynard Keynes wrote in 1921...

> Governments can confiscate, secretly and unobserved, an important part of the wealth of their citizens. By this method, they not only confiscate, but they confiscate arbitrarily; and while the process impoverishes many, it actually enriches some... Those to whom the system brings windfalls... become "profiteers" who are the object of the hatred... the process of wealth-getting degenerates into a gamble and a lottery...

You heard him right – a "gamble and a lottery." Total credit market debt in the U.S. rose more than 30 times since the end of the 1960s. As a percentage of gross domestic product (GDP), it went up from 150% to 350%. U.S. equities rose 12 times and are now bumping around near the ceiling.

Since the 1980s, wealth-building in America has shifted away from making things to financing things. And the 10% have changed, too, from bold captains of industry to clever lords of finance.

Fortunately, as the system degenerates, more and more people want information and advice about how to get the soup. They turn to the financial press. That's us! So to the feds, their shills, their lackeys, and their enablers everywhere – keep it up!

The Decline and Fall of America's Working Class

The decline and fall of America's working class is a subject that draws much interest.

Semi-skilled labor isn't what it used to be. From my simple calculation, it appears that in order to afford a typical new house and new car, a working stiff today would have to put in about twice as much time on the job as he would have 40 years ago.

"How come?" is the question most people ask.

It's Like Asking Yourself Out on a Date

A report at ZeroHedge tells us that since 2010, U.S. corporations have added more than $4 trillion in net debt. What did they do with all that money?

They used almost all of it to buy their own stock.

Prices are set at the margin. So even a little bit of extra buying can have a big effect on stock prices. Four trillion dollars' worth of extra buying – coming from the corporations themselves – could account for 100%, or more, of all stock market gains over the last four years.

Whoa. What kind of crazy finance is this?

In 2011, the S&P 500 traded in the 1,200 range. In the first few days of 2016, it reached more than 2,000, which represented a capital gain of about $6 trillion or $7 trillion. If our math is correct, every dollar of that asset-price increase was purchased at a cost of about $0.70 of additional debt.

Is that a good deal?

So it appears... At least until the stock market goes down. Then the balance sheet begins to sag on the left, where the debits are, and lightens up on the right, where the credits are.

Stock prices go down as well as up. But debt remains just where it was.

Borrowing to buy your own assets, like asking yourself out on a date, is rarely very satisfying.

In the case of U.S. stocks, the next phase will likely be a transfer of wealth from the stockholders to the bondholders. That is, the stockholders will own less of the corporation and the bondholders will own more. The value of the equity will go down. The value of the debt – relatively, and assuming the corporations remain solvent – will go up.

When Women Have No Use for Men

While rich men were asking themselves for dates, poor men were getting no offers at all. Their incomes, wealth, and self-esteem were falling.

But how could so many people actually get poorer during what should have been the most fabulously productive period in history?

And yet the figures – subject to much misinterpretation – and the anecdotal evidence coming from our own readers point in the same direction: The typical American man has less real, disposable income today than he had 40 or even 50 years ago. Surely, he must be feeling a little blue.

Here's what Professor Noah Smith says...

> One big piece of news in the past couple of weeks has been the release of a new paper by recent economics Nobel winner Angus Deaton and his co-author Anne Case. The paper

> highlights a very disturbing trend – death rates are increasing
> for white people in America, especially for working-class
> middle-aged whites. The increase looks like it has been going
> on since the late 1990s.
>
> ... for white Americans with no college education, deaths have
> soared...

Other groups of men – Hispanics and blacks – live longer. Why would
life expectancy be going in the opposite direction for whites? The
proximate causes, according to the Deaton-Case paper, were drugs,
alcohol, and suicide. But what's behind it... why?

In 1965, Daniel Patrick Moynihan's famous report on the "Negro
Family" warned that black families were being destroyed. Out-
of-wedlock babies, family breakups, poverty, drugs, violence,
unemployment, prison – blacks were actually falling further and
further behind whites, he noted.

But now it is poor or "middle-class" whites who are being left for
dead. They can't get decent jobs. Their marriages are breaking up.
Their children are raised by single parents (the rate is about the
same for whites today as it was for blacks in the '60s). They drink too
much. They take drugs. They've given up looking for work. They kill
themselves at a startling rate. Why? Smith guesses:

> The uneducated class became a floating low-skilled labor
> force, which decreased the marriageability of white working-
> class men. That impaired family formation. A couple of
> decades later, the lack of family support started to take a
> big bite out of the emotional health of working-class whites,
> causing them to turn to alcohol, drugs, and suicide once they
> reached middle age.

We'll take our own guess: As the "breadwinner" jobs disappeared,
white men lost their sense of purpose and place. Women often find it
easier to get work and often earn more. Men could no longer "bring
home the bacon." Women had less use for them.

But watch out. When women have no use for men, men soon get up to mischief.

What to Do When the 'Empire of Debt' Crumbles

"Dere's dem dat's smart… an'dere's dem dat's good," said Uncle Remus.

Many young people today can't even identify Uncle Remus. Some of their elders might want to arrest you for quoting him in the original dialect. But the man was a genius.

When we were young, we were a lot smarter. But as the years go by, many of the things we thought were smart don't seem so smart anymore. And now we realize that no matter how smart we think we are, we are never smart enough.

We think stocks are going up. We think we can build a better world in Mesopotamia. We think we can tell the fellow down the street how to discipline his children or decorate his house. But what do we know?

It is easier to be smart than to be good. That's why there are so many smart people and so few good ones. Smart men get elected to high office. They run major corporations. They write editorials for the newspaper.

Pity the poor good man. He goes to parties and has nothing to say that is not mocking and cynical. Others talk about their smart deals, their smart ideas, their smart plans and successes. Women crowd around them. A smart man grows taller as he speaks. The good man shrinks.

The Virtuous Path

But in economics and investing, it is virtue, not brainpower, that really pays off. "All the world is moral," said philosopher Ralph Waldo

Emerson. It is moral in the sense that if you are careless enough to step on a hoe, the handle will hit you in the face.

One generation takes the virtuous path. The next is likely to slip off, honoring the old virtues in speech, but not in act. The oldest generation of Americans remembers the Great Depression. They borrowed reluctantly, saved eagerly, and made the United States the greatest power on Earth.

Their children still talked their parents' talk but didn't mind walking off in a different direction when the wind was at their backs. And their grandchildren? The newest generation seems to have no regard for the virtues of their grandparents or the futures of their grandchildren. They disregard the wisdom of the dead and load up the unborn with debt.

The end of the U.S. Empire of Debt may be near or far. We don't know. Washington will probably not be sacked any time soon. But the imperial currency – the dollar – is in grave danger. America's central bankers not only fail to protect it... but they also invite the barbarians to destroy it... slowly.

How to Protect Your Wealth

It's as if the police had gone on strike and started holding up liquor stores and mugging pedestrians. Since the central bank won't protect your wealth, you'll have to do it yourself.

How?

The old-fashioned way: by packing heat – holding reserves of your own. Traditionally, what the central banks hold in reserve is gold.

Mr. James Surowiecki wrote a wise but moronic piece on gold in the *New Yorker*. His wisdom is centered on the insight that neither gold nor paper money is true wealth, but only relative measures, subject to adjustment.

"Gold or not, we're always just winning on air," he wrote. "You can't be rich unless everyone agrees you're rich."

In other words, there is no law that guarantees gold at, say, $450 an ounce. It might just be priced at $226 an ounce, as it was when George W. Bush took office for the first time. Since then, a man who counted his wealth in *Krugerrands* has become nearly 500% richer.

But gold wasn't born yesterday, or four years ago. Mr. Surowiecki noticed that the metal has a past, just as it has a present. He looked back a quarter of a century. The yellow metal was not a great way to preserve wealth during that period, he notes.

As a result, he sees no difference between a paper dollar and a gold doubloon or between a bull market in gold and a bubble in technology shares.

"In the end, our trust in gold is no different from our trust in a piece of paper with 'one dollar' written on it," he believes. And when you buy gold, "you're buying into a collective hallucination – exactly what those dot-com investors did in the late 1990s."

Pity he didn't bother to look back a little farther. This is the moronic part. While Mr. Surowiecki looked at a bit of gold's past, he didn't see enough of it. Both gold and paper dollars have histories, but gold has far more. Both gold and paper dollars have a future.

But – and this is the important part – gold is likely to have more of that, too.

The Trade of the Century

What is the best place for your money now?

Take a look at the following chart...

Investment Performance & World Debt

Source: Bloomberg, FRED, McKinsey, & External Wealth of Nations

When everything starts to go a little crazy

World Debt

Gold

Dow Jones Index

T-Bonds

Average Investor

GDP

www.stansberryresearch.com

What is it telling us?

We see the apparent truth of Wall Street's claim: In the long run, an investor is best advised to keep his money mainly in stocks. But when we look more closely, we wonder if it is true.

After the money system changed in 1971, we see two major periods. In the first, which lasted about 24 years, you would have been best off invested in gold. Stocks went nowhere. Bonds were crushed by inflation. Except for an unusually high CPI, there was nothing particularly unusual about that period.

Until 1995, nothing "went crazy." After that, everything did.

The second period, from about 1995 to today, was marked by a very peculiar thing... the kind of abnormality that the gods do not tolerate for long. Lines do not normally go up like that. And when they do, "reversion to the mean" soon becomes more than a theory. It becomes a reality.

On Planet Earth, we can find our direction by reference to the Magnetic North. For investing, we use the most reliable force in finance – the relentless return to "normal" – to get our bearings.

And searching for normal, we may have stumbled upon what could be the "Trade of the Century."

What Is Normal?

As economists describe it, reversion to the mean is merely a recognition of the tendency for things to stay in a range that we recognize as "normal."

Trees do not grow 1,000 feet high. People don't run 100 mph. You don't get something for nothing.

Normal exists because things tend to follow certain familiar patterns, shapes, and routines.

When people go out in the morning, they know, generally, whether to wear a winter coat or a pair of shorts. The temperature is not 100 degrees one day and zero the next.

Occasionally, of course, odd things happen. And sometimes, things change in a fundamental way. But usually, when people say "this time is different"... it's time to bet on normal.

This phenomenon – reversion to the mean – has been thoroughly tested and studied in the investment world. It seems to apply to just about everything – stocks, bonds, strategies, markets, sectors... you name it.

What is unusual in the previous chart? What is so abnormal that the mean is likely to revert against it?

Global debt was only $30 trillion in 1994. In 2016, it is $200 trillion. That $170 trillion in extra credit is probably the whirlwind that sent equities spinning up.

Those gusts blew stock and other asset prices up to heights never seen before. The Dow reached more than 18,000. Houses went on the market for more than $100 million. Gold rose above $2,000 per ounce.

But now, the wind blows in the economy's face... making forward progress almost impossible. The real economy – noted as GDP at the bottom of the chart – has grown in a rather normal way, but at a slower and slower rate.

Its steady, plodding increase gives no hint of the chaos going on above it. The real economy and the financial world are as different as the eye of a hurricane to the swirling clouds and storms around it.

Another thing you notice is that until the mid-'90s... and again between 2008 and 2012... the average investor got essentially no benefit in exchange for the added risk of putting his money into equities.

In theory, he is supposed to be able to earn some return – over cash – lending his money to the U.S. government (with the 10-year Treasury bond as the benchmark). He should also be able to earn a premium (more than he would earn from risk-free Treasurys) by investing in stocks. The premium is supposed to compensate him for the risk that his stocks could go down at an inconvenient time.

In practice, we find that risk-free Treasurys gave him less than nothing. He has earned less from Treasurys than he would have from gold (which pays zero interest) – over the entire 44-year period.

Stocks, meanwhile, earned him nothing for the first 24 years. Then they exploded to the upside, along with debt, until the 2008-2009 financial crisis brought them back in line with gold.

By 2008, the average investor was again earning less on stocks – despite all the risk and bother of market investing – than on gold. It continued like that until 2012, when stock investments began returning more than gold.

Since then – and this is just a hunch – all the average investor earned was probably not worth the risk.

The Investment Compass

I had lunch with French economist Charles Gave. About 40 years ago – when he was "still young and creative" – Gave described what he called the "Four Quadrants Framework" for figuring out where we are and what we, as investors, should do.

Like a map, the financial world can be divided into north, south, east, and west. Each place has its threats and opportunities. But to get where you want to go, you have to first know where you are.

Prices are either going north or south... and they do so in an economic world that is either moving forward or backward (east or west). I have adapted Gave's model in a way that must surely make him cringe... but it should help us understand and may provide useful bearings for our onward journey.

The first question to ask is...

Is the period we are entering inflationary or deflationary?

So let's ask: Are prices rising?

In general, consumer prices have been going up since the Fed was created in 1913. Since then, inflation seems to be a fact of life, like the prevailing winds on a small island. So it's not enough to know the wind is blowing. We also have to have an idea of the wind speed: Is it picking up or dropping?

With that refinement, we reach a conundrum perhaps unanticipated by Gave in 1978.

Consumer price inflation – as measured by the Consumer Price Index ("CPI") – has subsided from gale force in 1980 to almost nothing in 2016. At a CPI reading of 0.5% (including energy and food), hardly a leaf flutters.

Consumer Price Index (CPI)

Since 1980, consumer price inflation has been coming down

Source: Bloomberg

www.stansberryresearch.com

But while consumer price inflation has eased, asset prices have had a brisk wind at their backs the whole time. So the answer to what would appear to be the simplest question – inflation or deflation – turns out to be more complicated than I expected.

Since 1980, consumer price inflation has been coming down. But asset price inflation has hardly let up.

Which is it? Inflationary or disinflationary (i.e. a slowing rate of inflation)?

Gave proposes a good way to judge whether the financial world is rising or falling. He refers to the work of Swedish economist Knut Wicksell. Wicksell said there are two interest rates – the "natural" rate... and the actual rate, which must be "unnatural."

If the natural rate (what borrowed money should cost) is higher than the actual lending rate, the result is a boom.

It means that money is easier to get than it "should" be... so people tend to borrow and spend more... resulting in an increase in both the velocity of money and the quantity of it.

The result? Higher prices. More speculation. More investment. Booms and maybe even bubbles. If the natural rate is lower than the actual rate, money is hard to come by... which forces a general retrenchment in financial activity.

It seems so simple, doesn't it? But there's a problem: You know what the actual rate is, but you can never know what the natural rate should be. Trying to discover the natural rate of interest by looking at today's bond market is like observing escaped prisoners at an orgy in order to figure out how many times people naturally have sex.

Wicksell wrote at a very different time. You could discover the natural rate of interest just by looking to see where the offer of savings met a bid from a borrower.

Today, it's not possible because the banking system no longer puts savers and borrowers together. Instead, it peddles credit that is created out of thin air.

Today, no one needs to save a dollar for someone else to borrow a dollar. This makes the supply of credit almost unlimited and the price of it subject to manipulation.

There used to be an absolute limit on the amount of savings held by a bank, which pushed up interest rates quickly in boom conditions, thereby automatically cooling an "overheating" economy. That limit no longer exists. Banks can lend as much as they want, subject to regulations and restrictions.

But even without knowing the natural rate with any precision, we can be fairly sure that the actual rate of interest was considerably below the natural rate for the last 20 years or so.

Gave used a shortcut. He took the GDP growth rate as a substitute for the natural rate of interest, on the assumption that, over time, the two should converge.

That seems right, but I'm not sure if there is any real evidence for it. If the economy were growing at 4%, for example, it seems logical that interest rates would rise or fall to an equilibrium rate around the same level.

If you could borrow for less than 4%... while achieving a 4% growth rate in your business (in the aggregate)... you should borrow until the price of money is driven up to the "hurdle rate," the rate above which your business' growth can no longer cover the cost of borrowing. Once the cost of money is above 4%, you would desist from taking out loans... reducing the pressure on the borrowing side... until the price of money falls to a point where borrowing becomes cheap enough to make sense again.

It may be simpler just to admit that we can't know the natural rate. Still, any time you can borrow at less than the GDP growth rate, you're in an "easy money" period when the world of finance should be expanding. If GDP growth falls below the cost of money, the financial world will contract.

This sounds logical. And it seems to accurately describe the last quarter of a century. The Fed and other central banks favored cheap money over dear money. Faced with an economic slowdown, they quickly cut rates... but then, as the economy recovered, they were slow to raise them.

A broader way to look at the Investment Compass is to think of the north-south axis as measuring growth or shrinkage in the financial world or Wall Street, while the east-west axis applies to Main Street, the economy.

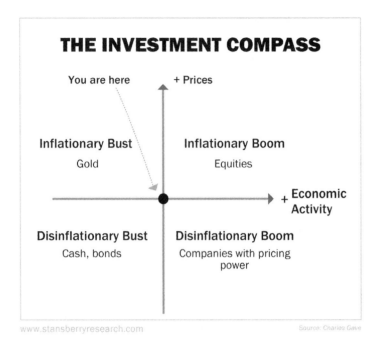

Source: Charles Gave

The popular view of inflation is that it only applies to consumer prices... When the price of a McDonald's hamburger or a ticket to a baseball game goes up, that's inflation. But when your stock prices go up, it's because you are an investment genius. The classic view of inflation was that it applied to the money supply, not prices.

"Inflation" referred to an increase in the quantity of money, which could manifest itself anywhere. This seems like a better way to look at it. And "money" today should include credit – the most common purchasing medium used in many countries. This further explains and describes what actually happened in the last two decades.

Since the mid-1990s, there has been a big growth of the money supply – especially credit – which expressed itself in the form of rising prices. Consumer goods, stocks, bonds, commodities, collectibles, and real estate all rose episodically. There were booms and busts, but the general direction for everything was up. Gradually, the rate of growth in consumer prices faded, but asset prices took over... with three major storms.

Again, 1995 seems like a critical year, when consumer price inflation gave way to asset price inflation, and a more or less "normal" financial world was shoved aside by a real weirdo.

Now, we are beginning to better understand those lines on our first chart.

George H. W. Bush lost the White House to Bill Clinton in 1992. Bush blamed Alan Greenspan for keeping money "too tight." Greenspan never made that mistake again.

His successor, Ben Bernanke, vowed – with a nod to Milton Friedman – to pump up the money supply rather than risk another depression. And Janet Yellen follows on the now well-trod path.

You can clearly see the Greenspan Bubble lasting to the end of the 1990s, then the Bernanke Bubble until 2007, followed by the Yellen Bubble.

And if you want to know why the performance of stock market investors in the second period was so much better than it was in the first, look at the "World Debt" line on our chart earlier in the chapter. Each bull market since 1995 ended with a steep break to the downside. In 2000 and again in 2008, both the markets and the economy tried to revert to the mean to correct the excesses of the prior period. And each time, the authorities rushed to save the situation with even more extraordinary measures.

For the third time in less than 20 years, it appears that markets are making a major attempt to return to normal.

The Southwest Quadrant

We have seen that even in the best of times, a generalized investment "in the market" is a bad idea. The gains that should have come to a stock market investor did not reliably appear.

For 40 years, there was no "equity risk premium" and no accumulated earnings. What happened to it? Perhaps it was taken by parasitic insiders. We don't know. But if that's what happens in the best of times, imagine what happens when the going gets tough.

What to do? Now we have established our present location as best we can. We are dead in the water, or close to it. The economy is barely growing or perhaps already in recession. Prices for assets and consumer items are either falling or flat.

And at least until the feds intervene in ways that are reckless and foolhardy, we're most likely headed toward the Southwest Quadrant – where we find all manner of woe, including falling asset prices, defaults, bankruptcies, and so forth.

The best place for money in this quadrant is **cash**. So that is our main holding. **Gold** is another main holding. What else? How can we position ourselves to take advantage of a return to normalcy?

We go back to our compass... back to the "return to normal." There is some cosmic law. What goes up must come down. We know that to be true. Is the opposite true, too... what goes down must come up? Can you reliably bet on it? It appears so.

Mebane Faber, the co-founder and chief investment officer of Cambria Investment Management, studied the phenomenon. He wanted to see when and how really cheap stock markets went back to normal.

For example, he looked at "cyclically adjusted price-to-earnings (P/E)" ratios (CAPEs). When they were less than seven – indicating extreme cheapness – the following year showed an average compound annual growth rate ("CAGR") of more than 30%...

FUTURE MARKET RETURNS WHEN CAPE RATIO IS BELOW SEVEN

	1 Year	3 Year	5 Year	10 Year
CAGR	30.9%	17.6%	20.5%	14.4%

Source: Global Financial Data

And it works in both directions. If you find a market with a CAPE ratio of more than 45, you will likely get negative returns in the five following years...

FUTURE MARKET RETURNS WHEN CAPE RATIO IS ABOVE 45

CAGR	1 Year	3 Year	5 Year	10 Year
	-8.9%	-4.1%	-0.8%	1.2%

www.stansberryresearch.com   Source: Global Financial Data

Another way to tell if a company is cheap is to look at its "Q" ratio, which compares its market price to the cost of replacing its assets. The higher the ratio, the more expensive the stock.

A study by Mark Spitznagel – the president and chief investment officer of Universa Investments – showed that higher returns came from companies with lower Q ratios.

Again, he found that traffic on Normal Street goes in both directions. Buying stocks with high Q ratios (expensive stocks) greatly increased the risk of losing money...

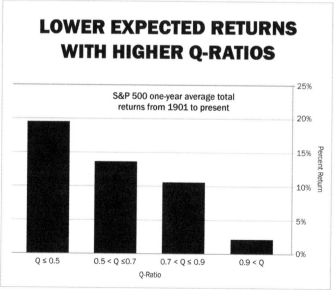

www.stansberryresearch.com   Source: The Dao of Corporate Finance

You can use cash flow, sales, profits, or dividend yield to measure "cheapness." But the results are always about the same: **The cheaper the stock (or the stock market), the better the returns**.

Dividends are important because they tend to be a big portion of your total return. The higher the dividend, the cheaper the stock. A stock that pays no dividends must go up, or you get nothing. A good dividend-payer, on the other hand, can provide you income even if the share price is moving horizontally or even down.

All this is to say that cheap is more likely to revert to normal than abnormally expensive is to become even more expensive. **Since we think we are headed south and west on the investment compass, we should heavily favor cash and gold, with lighter components of stocks and bonds**.

Keep in mind that our stay in the Southwest Quadrant is likely to be cut short by a quick move to the Northwest Quadrant, in which bonds and cash will be taken out and shot.

Cash is, by definition, liquid. You can exchange it for gold at any time. So the move to the Northwest (high inflation) Quadrant will give you time to put your cash to work without much loss. Good companies can usually survive high inflation, too. They produce things people want and need and can usually raise prices to offset their increasing costs.

But bonds cannot survive high levels of inflation. They lose their value quickly and don't come back. I don't want to own anything that I need to keep a close eye on or even remember to get out of. Personally, I own no bonds.

One side of the Trade of the Century would have us betting against that red line ("World Debt") on the chart at the beginning of this chapter. That is, you would short the financial assets that now depend on further increases in credit – stocks and bonds.

I'm not smart enough or motivated enough to short stocks and bonds. Instead, I'm short credit, just by owning gold.

From about 700 BC up until President Richard Nixon abandoned the gold standard in August 1971, gold was the world's "normal" money. The post-1971 dollar is abnormal. Holding gold is a bet on reversion to the mean, a bet that the world will return to the normal money of civilized life.

Then, you will probably get your reward as we move around the Investment Compass. First, the Southwest Quadrant will destroy the value of credit-fueled stocks. Next, the Northwest Quadrant will wipe out any money you have left in bonds.

Now What?

This still leaves the question: *What should you do with your money now?*

What can we learn from the charts in this section? What insight can we take away? Where is "normal"... and what will likely head in that direction?

For my own money, I'm sitting tight... in cash, gold, and long-term stock holdings, about a third in each category. My investment horizon is likely to be longer than yours. I don't mind if the current price of any of these things goes down 50% and stays there for years... as long as the real value doesn't go away permanently.

In that sense, the most worrisome part of the allocation is cash. Gold goes down. And then it goes back up.

Good companies, too, tend to underperform... and then to outperform. That is even truer of whole markets. Individual companies always go away sooner or later. Whole markets almost never do. One company loses market share and another gains it. One has good management and another has poor management.

In the aggregate, stock markets – like gold and commodities – tend to go up and down, but they rarely suffer permanent losses.

When cash is impaired, it tends to be impaired forever.

If the next two decades are like the last two, we're making a mistake. Two thirds of our money is in cash and gold. If stocks go up substantially, in real terms or more, most of my portfolio will be left behind. Neither cash nor gold will turn out to be a good investment.

On the other hand, 20 years seems like plenty of time for normality to assert itself. If the last 20 years have been absurdly weird and kinky, the next 20 should be more like they're supposed to be.

And in that context, cash and gold may be about as good as we can hope to do.

Bill Bonner's Top Ideas

- Earning money the old-fashioned, honest way is still your best bet... unless you've got the government or the central bank in your pocket.

- The economy is barely growing, or perhaps already in recession. Prices – for assets and consumer items – are either falling or flat. And at least until the feds intervene in ways that are reckless and foolhardy, we are most likely headed toward falling asset prices, defaults, bankruptcies, and so forth.

- Bill keeps his wealth in cash, gold, and long-term stock holdings – about a third in each category. He has a long-term investing horizon, and doesn't mind if the current price of any of these things goes down 50% and stays there for years... as long as the real value doesn't go away permanently.

LETTERS FROM

Doug Casey

Doug Casey is the founder of Casey Research, a financial publishing firm specializing in commodity and natural-resource investing.

Doug's book on profiting from periods of economic turmoil, *Crisis Investing*, spent multiple weeks as No. 1 on the *New York Times* bestseller list and became the bestselling financial book of 1980. Doug is also the author of *Strategic Investing* and *The International Man*, one of the most well-known books on financial and personal opportunities outside America.

He has been a featured guest on hundreds of radio and TV shows, including David Letterman, Merv Griffin, Charlie Rose, Phil Donahue, Regis Philbin, Maury Povich, NBC News, and CNN. And he has been the topic of numerous features in periodicals and newspapers such as *Time, Forbes, People,* and the *Washington Post.*

Doug believes the Greater Depression is looming. In this section, he lays out a four-point plan for maintaining your financial and psychological independence during the downturn. *"Instead of becoming a victim of inflation and other politically caused distortions in the marketplace,"* he says, *"you can profit from them."*

Money – How to Get It and Keep It

What would you do if some act of God or of government, a catastrophic lawsuit, or a really serious misjudgment took you back to square one?

Even if you are already wealthy, some thought on this topic is worthwhile.

One thing about a real depression is that everybody loses. As the legendary editor of *The Dow Theory Letters* Richard Russell once quipped, the winners are those who lose the least.

As far as I'm concerned, the "Greater Depression" is looming, not just another cyclical downturn. You may find that although you're far ahead of your neighbors (you own precious metals, you've diversified internationally, and you don't believe much of what you hear from official sources), you're still not as prepared as you'd like.

A good plan would be to approach the problem in four steps...

1. Liquidate
2. Consolidate
3. Create
4. Speculate

Step 1: Liquidate

Chances are high that you have too much "stuff." Your garage, basement, and attic are so full of possessions that you may be renting a storage unit for the overflow. That stuff is costing you money in storage fees, in depreciation, and in the weight of psychological baggage. It's limiting your options... It's weighing you down. Get rid of it.

Right now, it has a market value. Perhaps to a friend you can call. Or to a neighbor who might buy it if you have a yard sale. Or to some of the millions of people on eBay. A year from now, when we're out of the eye of the financial hurricane and back into the storm, it will likely have much less value. But right now, there's a market.

Even if most people are no longer wearing those "He who dies with the most toys, wins" T-shirts that were popular at the height of the boom, there are still buyers. But the general standard of living is dropping, and mass psychology is changing.

In a year or two, you may find there aren't any bids and the psychology of the country has changed radically. People will be desperate for cash, and they'll all be cleaning out their storage units (partly because they can't afford the rent on them).

Liquidate whatever you don't actually need – clothes, furniture, tools, cars, bikes, collections, electronics, properties, you name it. You'll be able to rebuy something like it or better for cheaper.

Just as important, you'll feel light and mobile, unburdened by a bunch of possessions that own you and weigh you down. It will definitely improve your psychology, which is critical to the next stage. And the cash it generates will be helpful for the rest of the plan.

Step 2: Consolidate

Take stock of your assets. After Step 1, that should be a lot easier because you'll have less junk and a lot more cash. You'll already feel more in control and empowered. And definitely richer.

But your main assets aren't money or things. It's the knowledge, skills, and connections you possess. Take stock of them. What do you know? What can you do? Whom do you know? Make lists and think about these things, with an eye to maximizing their value.

If you're light on knowledge, skills, and connections, do something about it. If you're reading this, you probably already live life in a way that builds all of those assets daily. But there's always room for improvement. Think the Count of Monte Cristo. Or if you're not so classically oriented, think Sarah Connor after she met the Terminator.

Part of this process is to look at what you're now doing. The chances are excellent there's a better and more profitable allocation of your time. Even successful rock stars tend to reinvent themselves every few years. You don't want to get stale. That leads to Step 3.

Step 3: Create

Remember, the essence of becoming wealthy is to produce more than you consume and save the difference. But it's hard to maximize value working for somebody else. And when you're given a job, it can be taken away for any number of reasons.

There is cause, and there is effect. You don't want to be the effect of somebody else's cause. You want to be the cause for everything in your life. That implies working for yourself. At least turn your present employer into a partner or an associate.

Perhaps go through the Yellow Pages (while they still exist), page by page, line by line, and see what you can provide as a service for the businesses advertising there. I promise you, they're all looking for someone to come along, kiss their world, and make it better.

Think like an entrepreneur at all times. Remember that there is an infinite desire for goods and services on the part of the 7 billion other people on the planet. Find out how you can give them what they want, and the money will roll in.

I've said many times that I believe you could airdrop me naked and penniless into the heart of the Congo, and by the time I emerged, I'd not just have survived, but I'd come out wealthy.

Believe me, I don't think wealth is by any means the most important thing in life. It's important, but it should be considered a convenience, not an imperative. Not that I'd *want* to be airdropped into the Congo at the moment. I've gotten a bit lazy. I have other interests, and you can't be everywhere and do everything.

But now that I think about it, if I wanted to make a real fortune today from a small base, I might prefer Africa to any other continent. As an educated Westerner, you can quickly meet anyone on an equal level much more easily than you could at home. If you have a reason that makes any sense at all, you can be in the office of the president within a week.

These countries are all plagued with incompetence and corruption. They need everything, and they're full of untapped resources and talent. This is to the great advantage of a foreign entrepreneur.

For your next vacation, book a trip to Cameroon, Togo, Gabon, Zimbabwe, or Angola. Go through the Yellow Pages in the capital and meet anybody who is anybody. The chances are good you'll come up with several deals in the first week alone. If you can't find the time, send your kid who's just out of school and idiotically thinks he may want to misallocate time and money getting an MBA. This idea alone should be worth a million dollars. Or as I would prefer to think of it, 700 ounces of gold.

But to an economist, money, like all goods, has "declining marginal utility." In other words, the more of something you have, the less you need or want the next unit. Of course, more is always better. But it's unseemly, even degrading, to pursue anything beyond a certain point.

When I was in Toronto once, I spoke with a Chinese friend who, I believe, is worth at least $250 million. As he waxed philosophic, he allowed that he didn't feel he really needed more than 30 extra-large to live exactly as he liked.

I agreed, in that meals in the best restaurants, as well as the finest clothes, cars, and houses only cost so much. And it's well within a conservative return on that capital, without ever even touching the principal.

Is it worth it to get more? Perhaps not, unless your interests in the rest of life are entirely too narrow. The point of money is to allow you freedom, not to make you crazy with getting more.

That doesn't rule out speculation as an avocation, however. More – everything else being equal – is still better.

Step 4: Speculate

You've got money. Now, you have to keep it and make it grow, because staying in the same place amounts to going backward. That's partially because the world at large will continue getting wealthier, even as the dollars you own lose value.

In the past, I've discussed why a lot of old rules for success are actually going to prove counterproductive over the next few years. Saving with dollars will be foolish as they dry up and blow away. Investing according to classic rules will be tricky in a radically changing economy. Most people will try to outrun inflation by trading or gambling. The markets, which are the natural friend of productive people, will perversely prove destructive to them in the years to come.

You'll know when the final bottom in the stock market has come: The average guy won't want to hear about the stock market, if he even remembers it exists. And if he does, he'll want it abolished.

Instead of becoming a victim of inflation and other politically caused distortions in the marketplace, you can profit from these things. Rational speculation is the optimum approach.

What to Do If You're Already Wealthy?

Perhaps, however, you've already covered all the financial bases to your satisfaction. I have several thoughts on the meaning of wealth. You may find some of them of value as prices of everything fluctuate radically in the years ahead.

First, recognize that wealth is a high moral good. Don't feel guilty about having it or about wanting more.

If you've already accumulated and deployed enough capital to allow you to jump off the golden treadmill, congratulations... Chances are high that you are an exceptional human being.

I say that because the moral value of being wealthy is underrated. I don't mean that in a Calvinistic way, in that Protestant theologian John Calvin believed God rewarded the righteous by making them rich.

But I do believe that productive people – people who work hard to provide goods and services for others – definitely tend to be wealthier than unproductive people. They deserve to be. And since we don't live in a malevolent universe, people generally get what they deserve. So yes, wealth is definitely one indicator of moral excellence.

Sure, some wealthy people got that way by lying, cheating, and stealing. But they're exceptions.

It's much easier to become wealthy if (in addition to having virtues like diligence, competence, and judgment) you are known to be truthful and honest. Those who automatically think ill of the rich are, at best, paranoid fools.

Put it this way: Rich people may lack some virtues, but they definitely have at least a few that made them rich. Poor people, on the other hand, lack some virtues and definitely have some vices that kept them poor.

I'm a fan of some aspects of George Gurdjieff, the late-19th to mid-20th century Russian mystic who was also a merchant adventurer at some points in his colorful life. He said that anyone who successfully employed at least 20 other people must be considered at least partially enlightened and a type of guru.

That viewpoint always resonated with me. Self-made wealthy people may not be saints, mystics, intellectuals, or even especially thoughtful or moral. But they've proven they're better than the average bear in at least one important way: They can create and conserve wealth. And they've thereby eased everyone's path to further accomplishments.

Second, figure out your purpose in having money.

Sure, money makes life easier. And it enables you to assist people you like with material things. But I strongly suggest that you not take too short a view on this matter. Accelerating advances in medical science are not only lengthening human life expectancy, but new developments now in the works have the potential to vastly improve your capability and health as well.

Is it possible to live to age 200, with all the wealth, knowledge, and wisdom that implies, while maintaining the body of a 30 year old? Not yet. But the prospect is on the horizon. It will, however, be available only to those who can afford it.

Computer scientist and futurist Ray Kurzweil makes a case that the Singularity is near, and I buy his reasoning. It would be tragic if anyone frittered away his wealth, thinking he wouldn't live very long, and then succumbed to a self-fulfilling prophecy, not because of medical difficulties, but because of financial difficulties.

Third, don't give your money to charity.

Entirely apart from showing a lack of both imagination and foresight, it's a complete waste of good money, pure and simple. Contrary to popular opinion, it rarely does any good. It often does great harm. The whole concept of charitable giving is corrupt and desperately in need of a complete rethinking.

Fourth, if you do care about posterity (who knows, you might be reincarnated...), and on the chance you don't make it to the Singularity, **carefully consider how to dispose of your estate**.

For one thing, there's no reason to automatically leave anything to your children – unless they deserve it. The notion that someone should inherit your money just because he shares your genes is flawed and thoughtless. The example of Emperor Marcus Aurelius leaving the Roman Empire to his worthless son Commodus should be instructive.

Wealth should be left to someone who is most capable of increasing it – at least if you want to benefit humanity in general. And yes, I'm aware that humanity in general may deserve absolutely nothing.

At a minimum, consider that memes are far more important than genes. It's wiser, therefore, to leave your wealth only to individuals (related to you or not) who will carry forth values you hold dear and are worthy of the wealth. If nothing else, make sure you disinherit the government.

Also consider that dividing wealth dissipates it and generally makes it less useful. If you have $1 million, you could leave $1,000 each to 1,000 people. But apart from the fact that it's unlikely anyone knows 1,000 worthy people, that much money is only enough for a modest vacation or a few baubles.

The larger the pool of capital, the more ways it can be used, the more creative power it has, and the more likely it will be conserved and used creatively. I favor the Roman system, in which one could adopt children of any age – but always after you could see what their character was. You might want to do that if your own kids don't make the grade.

The Bottom Line

If you want serious money, you have to get serious about money. You need to understand these fundamentals and never forget them. Don't let all the garbage reported in the financial media you read, see, or hear confuse you about what money really is.

Don't consume more than you make: *save!*

Don't spend: *invest!*

Education of a Speculator

Editor's note: Everybody hates "speculators." Whenever a commodity, currency, or stock market collapses... every politician and bureaucrat races to the podium to denounce "speculators." It's a dirty word... one Doug Casey is among the few to embrace.

Speculating, Doug says, is simply "capitalizing on politically caused distortions in the marketplace." And he says that in the face of pervasive government interference in free markets, virtually everybody will be forced to do it to preserve their wealth.

Few people in the newsletter industry are as qualified to address this topic as Doug. Over a 40-plus-year career, he has used his knowledge of markets to amass a personal fortune... And as a best-selling financial writer, he has helped many individuals do the same.

In the 2010 interview below, Doug shares "war stories" from his years of investing and some priceless lessons on speculating and "contrarian" investing – putting your money where the crowd is afraid to go.

Casey Research: Doug, a lot of our readers have asked for you to tell some war stories. What were some of your biggest wins and losses? What were the lessons learned?

Doug: Well, it may not all fit neatly under the rubric of "Lessons Learned," but I can tell you about some of the specific experiences that have shaped my career. There have been some great deals and terrible deals that I've been in, and just as many of both that I've failed to get in.

Casey Research: It's all part of what hedge-fund manager Victor Niederhoffer would call "the education of a speculator."

Doug: Vic's an old friend of mine. His book by that title – *The Education of a Speculator* – has some important insights... although he's mainly a short-term trader. I prefer to only buy things I can hold onto for a few months, if not a couple years. It gives you enough time to be right. And it doesn't clutter your mind up with random noise and fluctuations.

Casey Research: Indeed. Let the trend be your friend. OK then, where do we start?

Doug: Here's what I did to start really educating myself... Among other things, I read Harry Browne's seminal book *How You Can Profit From the Coming Devaluation*. That led directly to my first big score in the market.

I read that book in 1970, and I bought gold coins. More important, as it turned out, is that I bought gold stocks and had a wild ride from 1971 to 1974. I made a *lot* of money, in percentage terms at least, since I was just out of school and had almost no capital to start with.

I then launched my second business venture...

Casey Research: Wait, wait... There was a big slump in gold in the mid-'70s. Are you saying you bought early, before Nixon closed the gold window, and then sold at the top of that first surge, realizing gains before the slump?

Doug: Yes, I did. But it's not as heroic as it sounds. I had no crystal ball. I sold near that interim top to invest in my second business, which was a company to market precious metals to the public.

I have to say that I learned more painful lessons on that deal than I did crashing my Ferrari one time. Not only did I lose all the money I had built up, but I lost a bunch of money I didn't have. It took me years to dig myself out of that hole. I never declared bankruptcy, but I had significant negative net worth for some time.

Casey Research: That brings up an interesting point. You're a libertarian, and libertarians believe in the sanctity of the contract. That being the case, are there any moral grounds under which a libertarian *can* declare bankruptcy?

Doug: I've always considered bankruptcy to be the act of hiding behind the state for the purpose of defrauding your creditors. It may be legal, but it's unethical. There's increasingly only an accidental overlap between what's legal and what's ethical. But most debt today is owed to banks. I have to wonder, with the banks increasingly becoming creatures of the state, if the morals involved haven't become inverted in today's world.

Casey Research: It could be a moral positive to borrow money from the government and then declare bankruptcy to help hasten the state's own demise?

Doug: Could be. Inflation is well-known to corrupt a society's morals in many ways. It's a dangerous thing, a slippery slope, to start rationalizing why one needn't make good on debts. But that's what's happening all over the U.S., with people walking away from their mortgages and their credit card debt and declaring bankruptcy in record numbers. It's a trend that's going to end very, very badly.

What the state has done by increasingly insinuating its tentacles into every aspect of life is to completely corrupt society. Both the intended and unintended consequences are going to be ugly, because it blurs the morality of daily life. It's entirely perverse that defaulting on debts can even be considered as a good thing, and inversions like this are proliferating.

Casey Research: We should do a conversation devoted to ethics – someone sure needs to. But let's go back to the '70s. What happened next?

Doug: Well, I had to dig myself out of that hole, so I redoubled my efforts to earn money. One of the things I did to earn money at the time was to write my first book, *The International Man*.

Casey Research: And thus was born a guru...

Doug: Well, it was *Crisis Investing* a couple years later that really put me on the talk show circuit. The other thing I did back in the mid-'70s was to become a stockbroker. Have I told you the story of how I managed to buy precisely at the bottom of the mid-'70s market trough?

Casey Research: No, please do.

Doug: I became a stockbroker in 1976, which was fortuitous timing for someone who liked gold stocks. So sitting there at my office in Washington D.C., I got a call from a guy – his name was Elmer – who impressed me as being one of these rich good ol' boys.

I talked to him about what I thought would be good investments for him, and he said, "I'll come into town and put a little bit of money with you." The way he talked, I thought "a little bit of money" was going to be several hundred thousand dollars, at least.

When he came in, it turned out that he was an average Joe who rode in on a bus and really didn't have any money to speak of. But I put a portfolio together for him, worth about $2,500. It included a thousand shares of a stock called Grootvlei, a thousand shares of Bracken, and several hundred shares of Anglo American Corporation of South Africa.

Because gold had fallen almost 50% from $200 at the end of December 1974, Grootvlei and Bracken were penny stocks – substantial producers, but with high-cost and short-life mines – that were each yielding indicated dividends of about 50%-75%. Even Anglo was yielding something like 15%.

Casey Research: Those are amazing dividends.

Doug: It's incredible what you can get in dividends alone when a market is at a bottom – something people seem to have totally forgotten about today.

At any rate, the day Elmer came in happened to be the day that gold hit its absolute bottom for that cycle – $103.50, if I recall correctly – and also happened to be the same day there were big riots in Soweto, South Africa that made headlines in the U.S.

So Elmer gets hit with these two things at the same time, calls me back up, and says he wants to cancel his order. I said: "Elmer, this isn't Woolworth's. You can't really take the merchandise back." But rather than paying me for what he ordered, he hung up the phone on me.

Having entered the orders for the stocks the previous day, I had to ask myself what I would do about it. It was something of a revelation to me – it was clear that I was dealing with a typical member of the public, a representative of the public's mindset. I figured he must be the perfect contrarian indicator. In today's terms, I had to ask myself if I was just talking the talk or if I was willing to walk the walk.

So I journaled those stocks I bought for Elmer into my account and held them until I sold in 1980 or thereabouts. By then, I was getting several times, annually, what I paid for them in dividends alone. It was a fantastic hit, at least in percentage terms.

Casey Research: So it was an accident?

Doug: Yes, completely. I didn't know it was the bottom. I just knew the stocks were really cheap. I believed what I had told Elmer about those stocks, and I figured it was more intellectually honest to keep them.

It turns out that I was right. People didn't want stocks that were off 90% and yielding 60% – they figured there had to be something wrong. They'd rather buy something that has gone up 10 times, proving it has a good "track record." Track records are the best way to judge people, but the worst way to judge stocks.

Casey Research: I don't think I've ever heard of anyone picking the exact bottom of that cycle.

Doug: I got lucky, but it's a perfect example of why it's essential for a speculator to be a contrarian. You've got to believe in your thinking enough to buy when everyone else is selling, even with frightening images on TV, like the riots in Soweto.

That's why it's critical to have an understanding of economics, politics, and the technical details of various businesses. Only then can you hope to be immune from the blather you'll hear on TV and read in the popular press.

And when it came to gold, few people had a clue. I remember one politically connected investment guru of the day – economist Eliot Janeway – saying that if the U.S. government didn't support the price of gold at $35 per ounce, it would fall to $8 per ounce. He didn't have a clue. But he influenced scads of people.

Casey Research: That's a great story. What a pity for good old Elmer.

Doug: Yes. I have no idea what happened to him after he hung up on me, but I thank him for appearing at the right time. Elmer was completely ignorant of economics and the markets, but he nonetheless taught me a more valuable lesson than any teacher in four years of college.

Casey Research: So what happened next?

Doug: The late '70s were good to me, despite it being the worst time for the economy since the Great Depression – high unemployment, high inflation, and skyrocketing interest rates. I was making great money in my regular business, royalties from *The International Man*, fees from speeches and occasional articles – and putting all my savings into mining stocks and gold, which was on its way to $800.

I wrote *Crisis Investing* in 1978. It was published in 1979 and hit No. 1 for many weeks on the *New York Times* Bestseller list in 1980. Then in 1982, I wrote *Strategic Investing,* which was more focused on the stock market, Dow Jones-type stuff. I got a large advance, $800,000, from Simon & Schuster. That's a lot of money today, but was a lot more money back then. And it confronted me with the question of what I would do with the cash.

I can't say that I thought gold was done then, but gold stocks didn't seem as cheap. So I bought things like Treasury bonds, which were yielding 12%-13%, and electric utilities, which were also selling for 12%-15% yields, and other things I recommended in the book.

It's an excellent book, still worth reading today. I was dead right about the markets, even though I foolishly remained bearish on the economy – the markets and the economy are not at all the same thing.

Casey Research: That was at the beginning of the 20-year bull market for Wall Street.

Doug: Yes, it was my next big hit in the market. At the time, the [Dow Jones Industrial Average] was less than 1,000. I said it was going to 3,000 – which was an outlandish and outrageous prediction. Unfortunately, I didn't keep the things I bought long enough. I didn't think the bull market in stocks or bonds would go on anywhere near as long as it did.

I was gone by the time it hit 3,000. That was one of the biggest mistakes of my career. I didn't foresee interest rates dropping as long and as far as they did, eventually driving stocks and real estate to manic heights. I could have held on and done almost nothing else for the next 20 years, but I didn't. Nonetheless, I bought close to the bottom and held on for a good, long run.

Casey Research: So what did you do after cashing in, in the '80s?

Doug: That's when I started getting into the mining stocks you now cover. I liked their incredible volatility. But it took me a while to really understand the way the game was played.

Even though the third thing I wanted to be when I was a kid was a geologist, it took me years to get geologically active, so to speak. But no regrets. It was a great time to get into the field because there were some fantastic gold-stock runs in the '80s, right up to the Bre-X scandal in 1996.

I went out into the field, as you do now, building first-hand understanding for the fundamentals of the business. That's as opposed to treating these things strictly like trading sardines – which, of course, most of them are. But even so, you can trade them much more effectively if you have a solid grasp of the technical areas of the business.

And there's no book for learning this. There's really no way to learn how to sort the wheat from the chaff other than to get out there and apply boot leather, spend a lot of time talking to geos, learn the psychology of the players, and watch the economics of mining companies as they develop.

The '80s were really a period of learning for me, playing around with wins and losses, all of which prepared me to profit from the bull market of the '90s. It has been a wild ride, with resource stocks cyclically going up 1,000% and then falling 95% – again and again.

Casey Research: You didn't have the advantage we had of a Doug Casey who'd done it before and could teach us the ropes – and whose experience we can now draw upon at any time.

Doug: Yes, it really would have been helpful if I'd had a mentor... but I can't think of anyone back then who could have taught me what I needed to know. If there had been, I sure as hell would have sat at his knee and saved myself a lot of money and aggravation. But all that effort at self-education did prepare me for the 1993-1996 bull market, which was a wonderful, fantastic time to be in the junior mining sector. That was the time when I had the three biggest wins of my career.

Casey Research: Ah yes, the famous "accident, scam, and psychotic break."

Doug: Well, the scam was Bre-X, of course. I was introduced to that by my friend Rick Rule, who also introduced me to Silver Standard Resources and several other huge wins I've had in my career.

Bre-X was coming out with fantastic results from its drilling in the orangutan pastures of Indonesia. At the time, the stock was trading for about a buck, and there weren't too many shares out. I started buying, and the story just kept getting better, so I started buying with both hands. Who could have guessed that someone was salting the drill core?

I ended up with a large position. When the stock was trading over $100 per share, I finally came to the realization that this exploration play had a market capitalization greater than that of Freeport-McMoRan, which had already put billions of dollars into its Ertsberg and Grasberg mines. And it was paying dividends.

I asked myself what the point of holding on was, couldn't think of one, and sold on that basis. As you know, the whole thing was exposed as a fraud and $4 billion of value disappeared.

The accident was Diamond Fields, of which I was a founding shareholder, simply because I was a friend of Robert Friedland's. I did a second private placement in it later, based strictly on the diamond assets. That was an offshore Namibian diamond play that looked great, as so many of these things often do, but didn't work out.

The only reason that Diamond Fields went to more than $100 per share instead of near zero is because a couple geologists on a helicopter ride in Labrador, where the company was closing up shop, saw something out the window that looked interesting.

They landed on the discoloration, sampled it, and that led to the world-class Voisey's Bay nickel discovery. It was pure luck those two geos were flying over that place and happened to look down at that time.

The psychotic break was Nevsun, which is still around today and is still active in Africa, as it was back in those days. I did private placements in that stock at $1 and $2, with full warrants, and rode it all the way up to $20, where I sold.

I call it a psychotic break because there was a broker in Chicago, now deceased, who, for some reason, went wild and decided to put 100% of his clients' money into that stock. He personally took it to $20, after which it slid all the way back to becoming a penny stock, before this cycle breathed some new life into it.

This all just goes to show that even armed with the best intentions and expert knowledge, it's sometimes extraneous events that can make all the difference.

Casey Research: That underscores the importance of sticking close to the action, so you're not "out of the room, out of the deal."

Doug: Just so. Media mogul Ted Turner supposedly attributes a lot of his success to just going where the action is and letting the law of large numbers work for him. It's true. You've got to be out there. Just running on the nine-to-five treadmill is unlikely to result in anything other than mediocrity.

It also helps not to be too risk averse, not to be intimidated by volatility, to have a contrarian nature, and to be inclined to go places others aren't interested in.

Casey Research: So since we've recorded your three biggest wins for history, it would only be fair to record some of your biggest losses. Care to let one of those out of the bag?

Doug: It's funny – I tend to forget about those, actually. It's painful reliving them. Let's say I try to forget the incidents, while remembering the lessons.

Casey Research: It's just human psychology. You might think we'd want to remember our most painful experiences so as to never make the same mistakes again. But there also seems to be a tendency to push painful things from our minds to enable us to continue functioning at all. The unfortunate consequence is that people often repeat their worst mistakes.

Doug: That might explain why I've lost so much money on private deals. When you put money into a company at its founding, while it's still private, and it never goes public, you never get an exit, not even at a loss. The money just dies and goes to money heaven. At least if it was good money.

There are companies I bought decades ago that are, to this day, still not public. For all I know, they never will go public. I won't name names, but for all practical purposes, this is dead money. So I'm extremely reluctant to buy into private deals, although I can't help but look at them and still take the plunge occasionally. Some of these things that were deposited with brokers still show up on my monthly statements. Seeing them there is like getting poked in the eye anew every time, so I recently told the brokers just to delete them – the ones that I know are bankrupt, anyway.

There's a lot that can go wrong before a private company gains a listing on a stock market. As well as after...

Casey Research: But you still do it. We saw you do it once.

Doug: You're right, but the price was really, really cheap, and I knew the people involved. If I have high confidence that the people involved will do what they say they'll do, that helps. But it still needs to be at fire-sale prices.

Casey Research: Words to the wise, duly noted.

Doug: I'll tell you my best "woulda, coulda, shoulda" story. The stupidest failure to act in my career. A sin of omission, not commission.

One of the largest publishing companies in the U.S. was started by a friend of mine in 1979. At the time, I was just starting to publish my newsletter, the predecessor of the *International Speculator*. He said he'd like to publish it, and I said: "Great, because I'm not a publisher and I don't want to be one."

He said he'd sell me 10% of his new company for $10,000, with the idea that would be the seed capital for publishing the newsletter. I passed on the deal, thinking I was being a shrewd businessman.

Today, I estimate that my 10% share of the dividends would have added up to $3 million or $4 million over the years, plus my 10% stake would be worth $5 million–$10 million.

Casey Research: Wow. But… if you knew your $10,000 was going to be seed capital for the publication of your own newsletter, why didn't you take the deal?

Doug: Well, I had other offers from other publishers, and they seemed more experienced and stable. They didn't need capital to get the job done. My friend's company was private with no experience in the newsletter-publishing business, and I just didn't think it would work. I was simply, totally, dead wrong about it.

It's still a private company, but it would be one of the most productive pieces of my portfolio today, had I not been so clever back then.

And I've got to tell you that another of my best deals was, and still is, a private company. Believe it or not, it was a placer deal in Alaska…

Casey Research: You're kidding!

Doug: No! Talk about all the things you shouldn't do in investing: It was private, a placer deal, and with people I didn't know well.

Casey Research: Why is it that when you hear of a mining scam, it's so often a placer deal?

[*Editor's note: Placer mining is the dredging of rivers, sifting of sandbars, etc. for gold that has accumulated in dirt, gravel, sand, and other "alluvial" matter.*]

Doug: The same reason that so few are in public companies – there are just too many X factors. The first thing that happens is that when you get going, your workers see nuggets of gold, and those nuggets somehow manage to disappear.

More technically, it's really difficult to estimate mining reserves in a placer setting. The flakes and nuggets are inconsistently dispersed into pods. On the other hand, it tends not to be capital intensive, and values are easy to recover by simple gravity separation. But that also means most of them have already been played out by prospectors.

Placer is a fun thing to play with during your summer vacation, but typically is not commercially viable.

Casey Research: So... *Why'd you do it?*

Doug: It seemed like a good idea at the time... famous last words. Actually an old friend, who did know the people, urged me to. And it wasn't much money – not that that's an excuse for doing something goofy. Sometimes it's better to be lucky than smart, although that's no way to invest.

Anyway, I got into this deal for $20,000 back in the early '80s. That $20,000 got me 200 ounces of gold over the years, which is still on deposit with a major broker to whom they shipped it. The company stopped producing in 2001 at the bottom of the market when it was just uneconomic. But it's going back into production soon, so I may still get even more gold without putting another penny into the deal.

Casey Research: That's more than 10:1 on just the gold it has dividended to you so far.

Doug: Yes. The $20k was tax deductible, since it went directly into expenses. And the gold is tax free until I sell it – which I have no intention of doing until there's a better place for the capital. Perhaps U.S. stocks when dividend yields are in the 6%-8% range.

But there's actually another one, an opportunity brought to me by Jim Gibbons, a longtime subscriber who started a company called Seattle Shellfish. In spite of the fact that I'd grown to hate private deals, Jim's project looked good, so I invested some money. It's still private, but it's paying me about 30% per year in dividends, and they've been increasing.

Incidentally, he wrote a book with a lot of insights that are especially relevant now. It's called *The Golden Rule: Safe Strategies of Sage Investors*.

Casey Research: Sounds like a love-hate relationship you have with private companies. How does one even start to make a rational decision in that environment?

Doug: Well, they could start with my friend Arthur Lipper's book, *The Guide for Venture Investing Angels: Financing and Investing in Private Companies*.

I've had a lot more losers than winners investing in private companies, but almost everybody does. You just hope that the occasional winner is big enough to make up for the losses, plus give you a worthwhile, risk-adjusted return. What that means is trying to go only for deals that, in your subjective opinion, have 10:1 potential. Better yet, try to negotiate for some type of security to reduce your downside risk. A study of Arthur's books – and he's got several – is a cheap education.

Casey Research: Any other painful lessons learned to share?

Doug: Like I said, I seem to have pushed most from my mind... But maybe I should also say that some of my biggest winners have been outside the world of gold stocks and mining and in the world of real estate.

Casey Research: Ah, yes, real estate is the other great passion of yours we've talked about, aside from poker...

Doug: Spain was a good example. I bought real estate in southern Spain before Spain joined the European Union. That worked out well, not just because of the influx of tourists and money from Northern Europe, but also because the dollar was much higher back then, making it cheaper to buy all kinds of things for giveaway prices. All of Europe was relatively cheap at the time. I also bought in Hong Kong during a China crisis. Same in Argentina – but crises there come often.

Casey Research: Any trend-watcher who was paying attention could have guessed that after Generalissimo Franco took his long-overdue exit from our weary world stage, things must have been at or near a bottom for Spain.

Doug: That's right. Another "woulda, shoulda, coulda" story in real estate is that I was in South Africa looking at beachfront property back in about 2000. It was cheap at the time because the rand was about 12:1 against the dollar (the price of gold and other metals was down). Had I done that, I could have made 10:1 on some of those beachfront properties during the following boom.

Casey Research: So why didn't you?

Doug: I didn't want to live in South Africa. The problem with many foreign real estate deals is that if you're not going to be there and watch over things, you just don't know what's going to happen. You get squatters, rapacious town councils, and so forth. It's always messy, but it gets out of hand if you're not there. Anyway, gold and gold stocks were so cheap, I thought that was a better place to be. So there are a lot of big ones like this that got away...

Casey Research: Like that castle you could have bought in Rhodesia during the war for $85,000.

Doug: Sure, but things can go wrong just as easily as they can go well, if not easier. Twenty years ago, I was talking with investor and philanthropist John Templeton at his office in Lyford Cay in the Bahamas about real estate.

He told me he bought some land in Costa Rica back in the early '70s. That was a smart move on his part because Costa Rica was cheap back in those days. But his lawyer, who was an ex-vice president of the country, managed to defraud Templeton.

The master at this game lost $200,000, that's a lot of money back in those days. Incidentally, I'd met the guy who took the money. So you just have to be careful about making long-distance investments in real estate, especially if you're not going to use them personally or stay close to them yourself.

Casey Research: Hm. Speaking of real estate, we heard a story about you that perhaps you can verify for us. We heard that when you started speculating in mining stocks, you'd actually been wiped out or had little cash. So you took out a second mortgage or something on a house you had in Vancouver, and that became the seed capital for your current fortune.

Doug: I forgot about that – it's true. I bought that house in West Van, which had 900 feet of really beautiful waterfront, for just under C$1 million, when the Canadian dollar was about 65 cents U.S. I sold it at the beginning of the 1993 bull market because I was really tight after the late '80s bear market, and I just really needed the cash more than I needed a big fourth house.

So I sold it for C$2.3 million, when the Canadian dollar was at about 83 cents U.S. Today, the house would go for about C$15 million, with the Canadian dollar at near parity.

At this point, I definitely would urge its owner to hit the bid – whether he needs the money or not. Vancouver property is riding for a fall.

Casey Research: That explains a lot. You always say that people should never risk money they can't afford to lose on mining stocks – "the most volatile stocks on Earth." So it seemed strange that you would have gone deep into hock to gamble in the market.

But you didn't. You liquidated a non-core asset and remobilized your gains. You missed out on more gains on the house, but that move provided the capital for the three biggest wins in your career, which you just told us about. Sounds like a great move to me.

Doug: Another lesson learned that this brings to mind is that whenever I've made big gains in the market, I've made it a habit to invest the profits I've scraped back off the table into something that can't dry up and blow away.

Casey Research: Hence the emphasis on real estate.

Doug: Yes, though real property has carrying costs, and it's illiquid. That's the bad news. The good news is that it usually stays where you leave it. That's another advantage of salting away gold coins – you don't tend to liquidate them.

Casey Research: So noted. Any more lessons learned?

Doug: Well, I don't regret much in life, but the things I really regret the most – even more than the big losses I've taken – are the opportunities I've let slip through my fingers. It happens to everyone, and you shouldn't regret it too much, but they sure do smart. In most areas of life – not just investments – it's not the things you did that you regret, but the things you failed to do.

Investment-wise, for example, some friends of mine were founders of Digital Switch some 30 years ago. I didn't really understand the implications of the switch, no pun intended, from electro-mechanical to purely digital switching. So I passed on what could have been a *huge* amount of money.

The founder of AOL was also a friend of mine. I actually used to work for him at one point when I was in the brokerage business. He made a billion dollars on AOL, another boat I missed. Coming close but no cigar hurts sometimes.

Casey Research: So what's the lesson to be learned from that? I bet there are even more deals you were right to pass up.

Doug: Lots and lots of bad deals I didn't get in on, for sure. Which re-emphasizes the necessity of looking at hundreds of deals – just so you can afford to walk away from 99% of them.

One more thing: I don't think it's possible to overemphasize the importance of having a voracious mind, of letting your curiosity run wild into every subject and to every part of the world. To be a good speculator, you should have the broadest and deepest range of knowledge possible. If

I had known more, I wouldn't have missed Digital Switch or AOL – it was my own ignorance that cost me those opportunities.

It's good to be lucky – but luck favors the well-prepared. For speculators, that means having the widest range of experience and knowledge possible, so you can see an opportunity for what it is when it comes knocking.

Casey Research: Hence our company motto: "Intensely Curious, Focused on Facts." Great stories, Doug, thanks for sharing them.

Doug: My pleasure. My guess is that this decade is going to feature some of the most volatile markets in history. That's a good thing for those who are prepared and know what to look for.

Doug Casey's Top Ideas

- If you want serious money, you have to get serious about money. You need to understand the fundamentals and never forget them. Don't let all the garbage reported in the financial media you read, see, or hear confuse you about what money really is.

  Don't consume more than you make: save!

  Don't spend: invest!

- Believe in your thinking enough to buy when everyone else is selling. Have a good understanding of economics, politics, and the technical details of various businesses. Only then can you hope to be immune from the blather you'll hear on TV and read in the popular press.

- Whenever you make big gains in the market, invest the profits into something that can't dry up and blow away, like real estate. Yes, real property has carrying costs and is illiquid. That's the bad news. The good news is that it stays where you leave it and usually increases in value.

LETTERS FROM

Mark Ford

Mark Morgan Ford is an American author, entrepreneur, publisher, real estate investor, filmmaker, art collector, and consultant to the direct marketing and publishing industries.

Mark started his first business when he was 11 years old. In the decades since then, he has launched hundreds of moneymaking ventures, many of which are now worth millions of dollars.

He has also worked behind the scenes to create, develop, and establish more than 100 financial publications across the U.S., the U.K., Europe, South Africa, China, South America, and Australia.

Mark is the co-founder of the Palm Beach Research Group and the current editor of *Creating Wealth*. He has also written dozens of books on entrepreneurship, personal productivity, and wealth building – including *New York Times* and *Wall Street Journal* bestsellers *Seven Years to Seven Figures, Automatic Wealth for Grads... and Anyone Else Just Starting Out*, and *Ready, Fire, Aim: Zero to $100 Million in No Time Flat*.

The best way to become financially independent and grow your wealth for yourself and your children is to learn from someone who did it. In this section, Mark shares personal stories of how he took charge of his own wealth and instilled a culture of financial responsibility in his children. He also lays out the percentage breakdown of his own portfolio for 2016 – and the best ways to protect yourself from a down-trending market.

How to Become Financially Independent in Seven Years or Less

You are middle-aged. Your net worth is meager. Your income is barely sufficient to meet expenses... And those expenses are going up. The Great Recession is looming. Economists are predicting things will get worse. What can you do?

Should you give up your dream of retiring comfortably one day? Should you accept a future of an increasingly meager existence? Should you grow bitter and curse the powers that be for putting you in this situation?

Or should you take responsibility for your situation and make changes?

That last question was rhetorical, of course. But sometimes, I wonder if people really do understand their options. There are things that happen in life that we can't control. But we can control the way we respond to them...

I understand that when you are halfway through your life and barely making ends meet, it seems like the only chance to become financially successful is to win the lottery (either an actual lottery or the stock market equivalent of one).

So it may be frustrating to hear some rich guy from Palm Beach tell you that you can't quickly turn $25,000 into $1 million by investing in stocks.

But I believe – no, I am certain – that anyone who has modest intelligence and a positive attitude can become financially independent in seven years or less if he or she is willing to work incredibly hard.

You do not have to give up on your dream of being wealthy. You always have the ability to change your financial life. It will just take a bit of time and patience. And it will require that you change some of the thoughts and feelings you have about wealth and your relationship to wealth.

The first thing you must do is **accept the fact that you are solely and completely responsible for your current financial situation**. Before you react defensively, read that sentence again... I didn't say you are the cause of your situation. I said you are responsible for it.

By taking responsibility for your current condition, you also assume responsibility for your future. Nobody can change your fortune but you. And nobody else will. The sooner you accept that reality, the sooner you will shed the anger and blame and begin to feel financially powerful.

I'm not giving you a pep talk. I'm telling you the truth. I've done it myself, and I've coached dozens of people to do it, too. It is a simple adjustment of your thinking, but it is extremely powerful. It works instantaneously. Without it, you cannot move forward, even by a single inch.

The next thing you must do is **set realistic expectations**. I've had people tell me that they don't want to make 10% or 15% per year on their money. They think returns like that are "ho-hum." They want some incredible stock tip or some secret get-rich-quick technique. But when I hear someone say that, I think, "This person will never become wealthy."

Realize that 10%-15% is a high rate of return. Warren Buffett – the most successful investor of all time and one of the richest people on the planet – has averaged 19% on his investments over his entire career.

And realize that the journey to millions of dollars is earned $100 at a time. You must be willing to accept this fact to move your financial life forward.

Your financial life is like a train that has stalled. And right now, you want to be driving it at 100 miles an hour. But it can't go from zero to

100 miles an hour in no time flat. Inertia is against you. Be happy with 10 miles an hour now... and then 20... and then 30. This is how wealth accumulates: gradually at first, but eventually at lightning speed.

The third thing you must do is **thoroughly understand the difference between spending, saving, and investing**. With every paycheck you get, cover your necessary expenses first (bills, mortgage, etc.). Then put some money toward saving. And then put some money toward investing. Then and only then – after you have "paid yourself" – should you add to your "spending" account.

The fourth thing you must do is recognize that your net investible income (the amount of cash you have after spending and saving) is the single most important factor in determining how quickly you will become wealthy.

Commit to adding to your income with a second income. Make an honest count of the number of hours each month you devote to television and other non-productive activities. Devote them to wealth-building instead. Cast aside the comfortable shoes of victimization. Put on the working boots of a financial hero.

It's not fun to realize, in the midst of your life, that you haven't acquired the wealth you want. But the good news is your past doesn't have to be a prologue... unless you allow it to be one. You can change your fortunes today by doing the four things I've just told you to do.

You are only 47, not 87. You have plenty of time to increase your income and grow your net worth. Why do you assume all is lost, when – as any 87-year-old will tell you – you have a whole wonderful life ahead of you... a life that can be rich in 100 ways?

Why We Lied to Our Kids

A few years ago, my friend and business partner Bill Bonner asked me to speak to a group of about 50 old, wealthy white people meeting in an exclusive beach resort. He wanted me to discuss "the challenge of intergenerational wealth."

What the heck is intergenerational wealth?

It's the wealth you've acquired for your children, grandchildren, and maybe even your great-grandchildren.

The *challenge* is how to preserve it. History tells us that people usually squander any money they inherit. And if they don't squander it, their children surely will.

This is a serious problem for seriously wealthy people. But I believe it's a problem for middle-class people, as well.

It's not just about preventing your kids from throwing away the money you worked so hard to save. It's about preventing that money from turning your kids into the kind of adults you don't want them to be.

The experience of speaking to that bunch of 50 grumpy old folks gave me a number of new and useful ideas about this problem. I'd like to share those ideas with you in this essay.

The Downside of Helping Your Children

Let's be realistic: It feels good to give, and we want to think of giving as a purely beneficial act. (With a stroke of the pen we can make someone's life easier.) But giving away money – whether to your children or to strangers – often results in unintended consequences... some of them undesirable.

Giving money to your children – at any age – can make them wasteful. It might make them dependent. It might weaken their ambition and strip away their self-confidence. And the expectation of getting money from you might even make them greedy.

It's easier to understand this when our children are young. We recognize that giving a small child everything he wants is likely to spoil him.

My wife, K, and I were concerned about this 30-odd years ago when our children were small. We lived in Boca Raton, where high-income Baby Boomers climbed over one another in some fiendish, unspoken competition to outspend each other on their offspring.

Parents taught their grammar-school children to distinguish Hondas from BMWs. High school kids knew which of their friends' parents had the highest-paying jobs. Some of them felt proud to come to school wearing Rolex watches and Gucci shoes.

As our family CEO, K waged a war against this by having high expectations of our kids as students and as family members. She was strict with household rules and stingy with luxuries.

If our boys failed to maintain a B+ average, we didn't allow them to go out. Period. Before they could play on weekends, they had to work around the house. And the work was real: cleaning toilets and cutting the lawn.

We had no live TV. Video games were verboten. We never bought them clothes or toys when they asked for them. They had to wait for their birthdays or Christmas. But most of all, we expected our kids to be respectful to us and to others.

In other words, they were *part* of the universe, not the *center* of it.

K's approach worked. Our children were not spoiled. Although – I must admit – I had doubts at times.

Once, a few hours before picking up his date for the junior prom, I found my eldest son polishing the vinyl seat of the vehicle he was driving to the event: his 20-year-old, rusted-out pickup truck. (He bought it from his grandfather.) He worked away at it in good spirits, seemingly oblivious to the stuffing coming out of a large tear in the middle of the seat. I wondered if we had gone too far.

Now, I have no doubts.

The Inheritance Question

What about leaving your kids money after you die?

I have a friend who doesn't speak to his siblings because of a dispute over the distribution of his mother's belongings after she died.

I've heard my neighbor refer to her mother-in-law as a "selfish bitch" because, at 80, the woman remarried and began spending some of her money on her new husband. When my father left more of his property to two of his daughters because they were unmarried, it caused a resentment that lasted several years.

"Family fights among children after death occur in a large percentage of families," Tim O'Sullivan, an estate planning and tax attorney, told *U.S. News & World Report*. "If the No.1 goal is to create family harmony, then the estate plan ought to be designed in a way that preserves it. It's so sad to see what happens in these situations."

The last thing a parent wants is for the money he leaves his children to become a source of discord. And yet, it happens all the time.

This is precisely why K and I always lied to our children.

Whenever the subject arose, we told them – in clear terms – they would "never inherit a nickel" from us. We said we intended to spend all our money before we died. If we couldn't spend it all, we would give it to a charity. We told them that we expected them to earn their own money – that they weren't entitled to any of ours.

And we meant it.

Well, we meant the part about expecting them to make their own money. But we lied about the inheritance. Of course we're going to leave them our money – at least some significant part of it.

We lied because we were afraid that if they expected an inheritance, they might become less ambitious. And it seems to have worked. Our boys have grown into young men who work hard, pay their bills, and never ask us for money.

Another – Maybe Better – Approach

Meanwhile, my friend Bill and his wife, E, took a different approach. They avoided lying when their children were small by simply avoiding the topic of money. Talking about money – they taught their children – was gauche.

But then, as the children grew into adults, they began to talk frequently and openly about their money. In fact, they formed a legal structure designed to preserve the family's intergenerational wealth.

In preparing the speech Bill asked me to give on "the challenge of intergenerational wealth," I had a conversation with him about our different approaches. And it changed some of my thinking.

I told him what we had done and said that we were happy with the results. I also told him that now that my children were adults – and their characters were largely formed – I was having trouble *not* helping them.

And then we talked about the inheritance issue.

He was surprised to hear that our children still believed they would not inherit anything from us.

"How long do you intend to continue with this lie?" he asked.

"'Til the bitter end," I answered.

"So they will find out after you are gone that they have all this money," he said. "Just like that?"

"Right."

"And they won't have had any guidance from you on how to manage that money... how to work together to preserve and grow it... how to use it productively?"

That hit me like a ton of bricks.

My kids knew how to work hard. They knew how to enjoy their lives. But I now realized that one day, they would inherit many financial assets about which they knew nothing.

So K and I decided to have a family meeting. We made it a formal meeting and asked our family attorney to preside. At that meeting, we showed our three boys – for the very first time – the sum of our assets. And we told them that we intended for them to inherit some portion of that.

I am pleased to report that their first reaction was negative. "We don't need your money," they told us. "And we don't want it."

I told them that I was happy they felt that way. But like it or not, they were going to inherit a sum of money one day. And we had to start talking about what they would do with it.

Since then, we've had several more meetings. And those meetings are influenced by a publication and organization that Bill and his eldest son, Will, started. It's called – appropriately – The Bonner Family Office (BFO).

One big idea that we borrowed from the BFO concerns the purpose of inherited wealth. Bill doesn't believe in cutting up wealth among the children so that they can do with it what they like. He sees the wealth as an integral family asset that should function more like a bank.

Rather than inheriting lump sums of money, the children inherit an interest in the family fund. The purpose of that fund is to help individual family members enrich their lives... but how they do that must make sense.

Children can borrow from the fund. But if they do, they must return the borrowed money with interest. They can use the money to start businesses or pursue education, but they can't use it to buy sports cars or yachts. They also should help the fund grow in value. That way, when they die, it's larger than it was – large enough to help their own children.

As it happens, I had formed The Ford Family Limited Partnership 20 years prior to this, so we used that structure to accomplish these goals.

We've already used the partnership to extend two loans: one to help our eldest son buy a house and another to help our second son start a business. Without access to these funds, neither of them could have done those things.

Their credit may not be good enough for banks, but it is good enough for us. Having the limited-partnership structure allows us to provide a financial benefit to them without spoiling them.

Another thing we've done is include our children in a charitable project I started in Nicaragua a number of years ago. It's a community center that provides educational and recreational facilities for local people.

Originally, I saw this as a personal project – my own experiment in charitable giving. But now, by inviting the family to get involved, I've benefited in two ways: I have their help in developing the center, and I can expect that it will be preserved after my death.

Our youngest son took over as director of the center two years ago. He's done a great job of it, hiring capable people and vastly improving the scope and quality of services. He receives a stipend for doing this. In addition, he's learning how to manage a somewhat complicated business with 20 employees and hundreds of "customers." (He asks me questions and sometimes listens to my answers.)

The Ford Family Limited Partnership owns rental real estate, which seems to be the perfect vehicle for our purposes. And recently, our second son agreed to manage those properties. As a musician and composer, he had little exposure to real estate investing or business management. But he's taken to it like a duck to water.

He spends several hours each week learning about the real estate business, learning that – like the music business – it can be both fun and challenging. Like our youngest son, he receives compensation for his efforts. This gives us a way to help him out financially that is merited rather than entitled.

Our oldest son hasn't gotten involved in any of the family businesses, but perhaps he will one day. If not, there's always the chance that a cousin or grandchild might want to get involved.

We still have plenty of assets to figure out, but we are comfortable with what we have done so far.

The community center in Nicaragua is fast becoming a project we all feel proud to contribute to. And the real estate business has already become a cool little private bank that can make loans to family members while it grows its asset base steadily and safely.

In general, I feel like we're doing a smart thing: involving our children in the management of the assets that they will one day inherit while we are still around to provide advice and guidance.

So what have we learned about this complicated subject?

While your children are young...

- Don't buy them expensive things just because you were poor and never had them. Remember that giving your children less is sometimes giving them more.

- Expect them to work – and not just at their education. Give them menial household chores and pay them fair market value for their work. Never overpay them.

- Avoid discussions of family wealth. If the subject of inheritance comes up, tell them they aren't getting anything.

When your children leave home...

- Make it clear that their bedroom is no longer their bedroom. Put their personal effects in storage. Tell them they are welcome to come home for brief periods as a guest. Remind them that guests are always well-mannered.

When your children become adults...

- After your children have proven to you that they can take care of themselves, you can begin to discuss family wealth, including what they might one day inherit.

- Consider putting a business or some income-producing assets into a legal structure that can operate as a family bank, making loans to them when merited.

- Consider establishing a family charity (if you believe in charity).

- Use the family bank and charity to teach your adult children what you have learned about managing wealth.

Your Wealth-Creation Playbook for 2016

Nine out of 10 people who subscribe to investment publications do so for two reasons:

1. To try to figure out which way the stock market is heading (up or down).
2. To discover a great new stock that will make them rich.

Does that describe you?

Be honest.

If so, you need to hear this: You are unlikely to accomplish either of those aims. Not now. Not ever.

The stock market is not a machine whose movements are mechanical and, therefore, can be studied and accurately predicted. Nor is it a single organism whose habits can be observed and predicted.

It is a digital record of an integrated ecosystem of thousands of individual businesses populated by millions of owners, vendors, and customers – most of whose buy and sell decisions are based not on predictable rational responsiveness but rather on emotional instincts and impulses.

If you insist on making financial decisions based on future-guessing, you will be right some of the time and wrong some of the time. But as Nassim Taleb persuasively argues in his book *Antifragile*, when most people get it wrong, they get it very wrong, often wiping out any gains they may have made while getting it right.

As for finding the next Apple – well, the likelihood of that is similarly slim. The data here are dispositive. The vast majority of individual investors (who try to beat the market by buying individual stocks) underperform market averages.

So if you can't reasonably expect to get rich by reading *The Wall Street Journal* and subscribing to *Hot Stock of the Month Newsletter*, what can you do?

You can model your investing behavior on the behaviors that have been proven, time and time again, to actually work.

Let's focus on the one behavior that is probably the most important...

I'm talking about asset allocation.

Asset allocation is the process by which you spread your wealth. In other words, you determine how much money you invest in stocks, bonds, real estate, gold, etc.

You might think that something so dull as asset allocation couldn't possibly be that important in acquiring wealth, but numerous studies have shown that it may be the most important factor.

In a 2000 study, Roger G. Ibbotson and Paul D. Kaplan looked at 10 years of returns for 94 mutual funds and 58 pension funds. They confirmed that asset allocation explained about 90% of the period-to-period variability of a portfolio.

Meanwhile, an earlier formative study titled "Determinants of Portfolio Performance II: An Update" found that asset allocation explained 91.5% of the variation in returns.

I like making important decisions not based on the logic of what I read but rather on the results I've personally experienced.

Sometimes, the two come together happily, as they do in this case, with respect to the importance of portfolio allocation.

When I was young and just beginning to make money, I had a persuasive conversation with a woman who convinced me to put all my spare money in a single investment that seemed sure to skyrocket in no time. It turned out to be a double disaster. Not only did I lose all the money I initially invested, but I also lost another five or six times that amount before I could get out.

My decision that day comprised several mistakes...

1. Trusting someone I hardly knew.

2. Being persuaded by logic when I had no personal knowledge of the investment.

3. Putting all my financial eggs into one basket.

This was an early but unforgettable lesson for me. It taught me, surely and definitively, that you can go broke – and you can even go into debt – by putting all or most of your wealth into a single asset class.

(This is why so many millions of Americans lost all their retirement savings and became debtors after the 2008 bank-created and government-supported real estate Ponzi-scheme collapse.)

Because of this early disaster, I became thereafter a compulsive diversifier of practically every dollar I could save, putting some of it in bonds, some in stocks, some in cash, some in real estate, and so on.

In 2000, when I "retired" for the second time to devote most of my time to writing, I created *Early to Rise*, a daily e-newsletter devoted to "health, wealth, and a life well lived."

Almost from the first issue, readers were asking me what "secrets" I'd used to go from broke to... well, there's not a way of saying this without sounding crass, so I'll just say it: rich. I was pretty damn rich.

But I was also uninterested in making any more money. I had plenty, and if I was going to write about wealth building, I was going to tell people the truth – or at least my truth – and not what I knew they wanted to hear. ("Which way is the stock market going? What's the next hot stock?")

To answer those questions honestly, I pulled out my old tax returns and bank account statements and looked at what I had done with my income over the years.

What I discovered was that I had made hundreds of individual financial decisions – buy this, sell that. Some of them were good. A few of them were bad. Most of them were in-between.

It wasn't the particular decisions that mattered but rather the general decisions about asset allocation (how much money to put into which particular asset classes).

So I began telling *Early to Rise* readers about my own asset-allocation decisions. At that time, there were only a few: bonds, real estate, a bit of stocks, and cash. But as time went on, I added other assets to the mix.

Back then, **I had invested the largest percentage of my money (it might have been 60%) into municipal bonds**. They were earning 6%, and they were safe (at that time, not so much later). My strategy was always to hold them to maturity. That strategy worked well over what was, at that time, a 15- or 16-year time span.

I had invested the second-largest percentage of my money in real estate. I owned two personal homes and partial interest in perhaps a half-dozen commercial buildings that were rented to companies I owned.

I also owned a dozen or so residential homes and condos, undeveloped land, a direct interest in several overseas development deals, and a half-dozen investments in limited partnership deals that developed residential communities. Although some categories did better than others, all of my real estate investing was profitable.

The real estate gave me (I'm guessing now) about a 6%-8% return.

(I got a huge, additional return from 2000 to 2005 and got out unscathed before the 2008 crash.)

Third on my asset-allocation list at that time were annuities and life insurance products. I later mostly came to regret these.

Since I stuck to a "no-load" index fund, the returns I got on that fund were equal to the market, less fees and commissions. I haven't calculated what they were, but given that it was a no-load fund, I'd say I probably did about 1% less than the market. Not bad.

In fourth place was money I had put into stocks. Since I had been an insider in the investment-publishing business for 18 years at the time, the only stock investing I would do was the safest for people who know they know nothing about stocks. I had a little more than $1 million in an index fund.

And **finally, I had put a relatively small amount of the money I had earned over that time into up-and-coming entrepreneurial businesses**.

Interestingly, this category gave me, by far, the biggest rate of return. (I believe this was because I knew and understood these businesses and was able to select and/or influence management, marketing, etc.) My return on those investments has been huge.

That was the situation in 2000. From 2000 until 2011, when I stopped writing for *Early to Rise* and began writing *Creating Wealth*, I continued to buy assets, but my priorities changed.

I was a heavy buyer of real estate from 2000 to 2005, got out the next year, and went back in, as strongly as I could, in 2010.

Since bond rates were dropping, I stopped buying them.

The way to wealth is through asset allocation – but not just with stocks, bonds, and cash. You need to put your money into a wider group of assets that will give you a full range of income and appreciation potential.

When it comes to identifying what those assets should be, I can only tell you what I've done and how that worked out for me so you can decide what is best for you.

So here it is, a bird's eye view of my own asset allocations in 2016...

Strategic Breakdown of My 2016 Positions

Direct Investments in Entrepreneurial Businesses: 40%

As I mentioned earlier, I originally put the smallest percentage of my portfolio into entrepreneurial businesses. But since I earned the highest rate of return from that category, it's now the largest part of my portfolio.

My total investment in this class was probably less than 2% of my current net worth, but it has grown to where it is today. That's why I'm such a fan of this category.

Real Estate: 28%

Real estate was once my first and worst single investment, but it has since become my favorite asset class, even though it ranks second in creating wealth for me.

I put real estate on top of the list for many reasons: It's real. It's tangible. It's sometimes lovely to look at. It gives pride of ownership. And most of all, it's the kind of investment you can leverage with safety (if you follow some basic rules) and make money from without spending much time.

I've learned a lot about real estate investing over the past 30 years. My current portfolio reflects that. It's comprised of income-producing residential units, income-producing commercial units, land banking (agricultural tracts, islands, and vacant lots), and investments (both direct and through limited partnerships) in residential developments, resorts, hotels, and office buildings in the U.S. and overseas.

Stocks: 10%

Although 10% might be considered small by conventional financial-planning standards, I'm happy with this percentage. Sixty-five percent of the stocks I own are "legacy"-type stocks – super-big, super-safe, dividend-paying, long-term businesses.

Ten percent of my stock allocation is in "performance"-type stocks – a selection of stocks that attempts to beat the market. Twenty percent of my stock allocation is in options – selling puts. And 5% of my stock allocation is in a combination of strategies that I consider to be somewhat risky.

Of the money I have in stocks, 5% is in options. That, therefore, is a small amount of my overall net worth. Although I'm currently decreasing the number of options contracts sold, I'd consider adding to my position in the coming year.

Bonds: 7%

As I mentioned earlier, bonds represented 60% of my net worth at one time (when I had only stocks, bonds, and cash in my portfolio). By 2000, that percentage was down to about 25%, mostly because my real estate and business investments had grown so much. Since I stopped buying bonds, they've dwindled to 7%, which feels about right to me. (I will buy bonds again someday. I love income-producing debt.)

Collectibles: 5%

I get the greatest pleasure from my collections of investment-grade art, first-edition books, rare cognacs, vintage cars, etc. But I can't pretend that they can equal, in terms of purely financial rewards, some of my other investments. The main drawback of collectibles is that they don't produce income. And I love income. But the benefit of collectibles – besides the lifetime of pleasure they can give you – is that they are tangible, portable, and non-reportable.

Life Insurance and Annuities: 4%

As I said in this essay, I generally don't like any kind of investment based on life insurance – annuities included. But after a great deal of research, I've found two exceptions that work for my portfolio. I encourage you to look closely into the sector before choosing one for yourself.

Cash: 3%

Around 2005, when it became impossible for me to find real estate deals that I could get for a gross rent multiplier (the ratio of the price of real estate to its monthly rental income) of eight or below, I started accumulating cash. When I went back into the real estate market in 2010, the cash portion of my net wealth was nearing 10%. That left me with lots of cash at a time when real estate prices were dirt-cheap.

I call this my "Cash Opportunity Fund." I got this idea from Tim Mittelstaedt, our editorial director at *The Palm Beach Letter*. He advocates keeping a store of cash that you add more money to every year. Then, when the crash comes, you will be able to use this fund to swoop in and buy a bunch of great assets at bargain prices.

Gold (and Other Precious Metals): 3%

I bought a bunch of gold when it was priced at about $400 per ounce. It has gone way up and come back down since then. But at 3% of my portfolio, it's still about 50% more than I need.

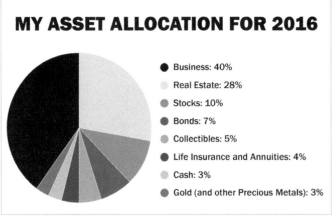

MY ASSET ALLOCATION FOR 2016

- ● Business: 40%
- ○ Real Estate: 28%
- ● Stocks: 10%
- ● Bonds: 7%
- ○ Collectibles: 5%
- ● Life Insurance and Annuities: 4%
- ○ Cash: 3%
- ● Gold (and other Precious Metals): 3%

www.stansberryresearch.com

Mark Ford's Top Ideas

- Accept the fact that you are solely and completely responsible for your current financial situation. By taking responsibility for your current condition, you also assume responsibility for your future. Nobody can change your fortune but you. And nobody else will. The sooner you accept that reality, the sooner you will shed anger and blame and begin to feel financially powerful.

- Buy real estate. It's real. It's tangible. It's sometimes lovely to look at. It gives pride of ownership. And most of all, it's the kind of investment you can leverage with safety (if you follow some basic rules) and make money from without spending much time.

- Discover collectibles that you like. Mark likes investment-grade art, first-edition books, rare cognacs, vintage cars, etc. But don't pretend that they can equal, in terms of purely financial reward, some other investments. The main drawback of collectibles is that they don't produce income. But the benefit, besides the lifetime of pleasure they can give you, is that they are tangible, portable, and non-reportable.

LETTERS FROM

Dr. Steve Sjuggerud

Dr. Steve Sjuggerud specializes in safe, unique, alternative investments overlooked by Wall Street. He believes that you don't have to take big risks to make big returns. And he has proven this to be true, time and time again.

Before joining Stansberry Research in 2001, Steve worked as a stockbroker, a hedge-fund manager, and the vice president of a global mutual fund.

Over his career, Steve has addressed dozens of financial conferences in the U.S. and around the world, including the New York Stock Exchange. He has also been quoted by the *Wall Street Journal*, *Barron's*, and the *Washington Post*.

At Stansberry Research, Steve is the editor of *True Wealth*, which uses a simple investment mantra... buy things that are cheap, hated, and in an uptrend. This simple strategy has consistently led to large returns with little risk.

Steve is also the editor of *True Wealth Systems*, which uses a powerful data system – something typically found only at hedge funds and Wall Street banks – to pinpoint the sectors most likely to return 100% or more.

In the next couple essays, Steve introduces two incredible opportunities to get a huge portion of your wealth out of the U.S. dollar before the impending currency crisis arrives. These opportunities could lead to triple-digit gains... and are historically proven to maintain and even increase value as the dollar declines.

The 'Perfect Hedge' Against a Weakening Dollar

There's an unbelievable opportunity to make five to 10 times your money... thanks in part to Washington's out-of-control spending.

And a lot of smart investors are already taking advantage of it.

This investment opportunity has nothing to do with stocks, bonds, or options. But it's in a market that's almost as big as the U.S. stock market.

I call it the "Perfect Hedge."

You see, the U.S. has managed – and continues to manage – its finances foolishly. As a result, our country's debt situation is worse than you can even imagine.

> By 2033, two things alone will eat up ALL government revenues: entitlements and the interest on the national debt...

This estimate comes from the government – the Congressional Budget Office – based on what it sees as the likely scenario. And it doesn't include "governing" expenses, such as bills, lawmaking, military, repairs to roads and bridges, and education. Add those in, and the U.S. quickly looks worse than the banana republics that have defaulted on debts in the past.

But Washington won't let the U.S. default on its debts. Instead, it will "inflate" them away through money printing.

Folks are beginning to lose confidence in the U.S. dollar. It's not hard to see why...

The Federal Reserve has repeatedly stated it will print money – as much as necessary – to stimulate our economy. The obvious result is more paper dollars out there. And the next result is that a paper dollar is worthless.

Unless we see some dramatic changes in government spending, *a major U.S. crisis appears inevitable.*

But before the crisis arrives, you need to get a huge portion of your wealth OUT of the U.S dollar… and INTO investments that will maintain and increase their value as the dollar declines.

In 2016, there's an incredible opportunity to take advantage of Washington's destructive financial policies and pocket gains of 100% or more…

This Is the Best Time in History to Buy a House in America

You may be surprised to realize that getting a mortgage is the perfect way to "hedge" the weakening dollar. When you borrow dollars to buy a house, you are essentially betting against the dollar and betting on the property.

If things go badly in America – if the dollar continues to weaken, if our politicians keep spending, if the national debt and taxes go up – housing will at least hold its value and most likely will go up.

2016 happens to be the best time in history to make this investment.

Fact No. 1: Mortgage rates hit their lowest levels in American history in 2013.

Most investors have only seen a couple decades of mortgage rates on a chart. But my friends at Global Financial Data have databases – including real estate data – that go back centuries.

Take a look at this chart of mortgage interest rates since 1900…

U.S. Mortgage Rates

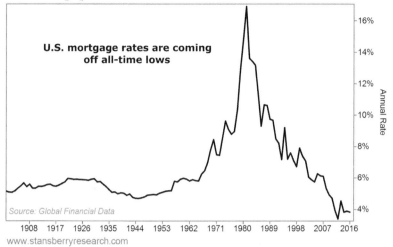

As you can see, mortgage rates hit their lowest levels in U.S. history in 2013.

When were mortgage rates even close to this low in the past? Just after World War II...

And what happened just after World War II? We saw the greatest post-war boom in housing prices – by far.

Mortgage rates bottomed in the mid-1940s, and house prices bottomed at about the same time. Then the greatest boom in home prices in our lifetimes started. Housing more than doubled in value over the next 10 years – from the mid-1940s to the mid-1950s.

Today, we are coming off record-low mortgage rates. And we have another thing in our favor...

Fact No. 2: In 2013, homes became more affordable than ever.

Based on the 30-year history of the Housing Affordability Index, houses recently became more affordable than ever. (The higher the index rises, the more affordable housing is.) Take a look...

Housing Affordability Index

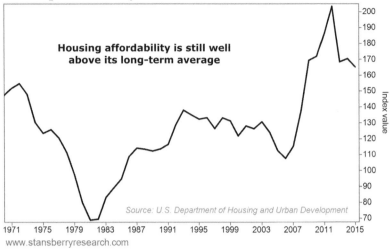

Housing affordability is still well
above its long-term average

Source: U.S. Department of Housing and Urban Development

www.stansberryresearch.com

"Affordability" takes three factors into account: home prices, your income, and mortgage rates.

The basic idea is simple. What do people think about when they buy a house? It's not the *price* of the house, really… It's the *payment*. People think, "Can I afford this mortgage payment on my monthly income?"

When mortgage rates hit 20% in the early 1980s, monthly house payments were ridiculously high… It was the least affordable time in American history. The second least affordable time in American history was at the peak of the housing bubble in 2006.

But home prices have crashed. They're cheap now! And mortgage rates recently hit record lows. Since household incomes nationwide haven't fallen nearly as much, homes are more affordable than ever.

Home prices have fallen by one-third… And mortgage rates are the lowest in history. Therefore, U.S. homes are more affordable than they've ever been.

Based on these facts alone, now is the best time in American history to buy a house.

I don't think we will ever see an opportunity this good again in U.S. housing... Not in my lifetime.

Brett Eversole – my lead analyst at *True Wealth* – took me up on this idea...

Brett bought his first house in mid-2013. It's a perfect example of what's possible. He bought a four-bedroom home here in Florida, close to the beach. The home was relatively new, with all the high-end features. It's in a nice, quiet neighborhood. And it has a big yard in the front and back. No neighbors behind him... just woods.

Get this – Brett paid $280,000 for it and got a 30-year mortgage with an interest rate of 3.5%! How great is that? It's a deal Brett will end up telling his kids about someday.

I've been "pounding the table" on real estate for the past few years. The good news is... you haven't missed it!

Yes, prices are up. And yes, mortgage rates are up. But you haven't missed it yet. Right now is still an incredible moment to buy/own property.

I have two secrets for you that will allow you to succeed in property now that the market has moved up...

1. Don't get stuck on getting the lowest price.

I believe a "fair price" today will turn out to be a great price in hindsight... a few years from now. Don't miss out on a great property because of a small percentage difference in your negotiation. There's no need to try to win the lowball game only to miss out on a great opportunity.

2. Buy the good stuff now even though it has moved up in price.

There's no need to guess which neighborhood is the next "up and coming" area... The areas that are *already good* are still a great value even though they're up... They will go up more as the housing market recovers. They are a smarter buy.

Even though prices and mortgage rates have moved up, the upside potential in housing right now is still incredible...

Most housing experts don't understand the "relative value" of real estate today versus other assets... They don't take into account that the bank pays zero interest... so there's nothing left out there for people to do with their money! Who wants to earn zero interest on paper money in the bank when you can own a real asset that can pay you rent?

In 2006, we saw how high housing prices can go. I expect we'll see something similar now. Most people don't trust stocks or their banks anymore. But they do trust a real asset they can control, like a house.

Your downside risk is also limited because a house can't go bankrupt like a company can.

Your upside potential is also incredible, by the way... even if interest rates are going up...

Interest rates in the 1970s shot up – from 7.5% to near 15%. House prices went straight up, too. Take a look:

Existing U.S. Home Prices (1970s)

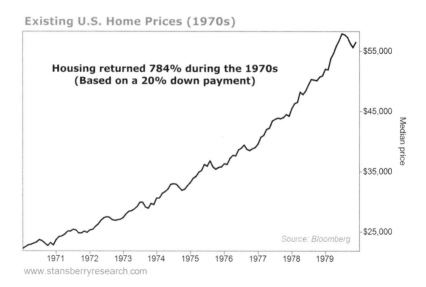

Housing returned 784% during the 1970s
(Based on a 20% down payment)

Source: Bloomberg

www.stansberryresearch.com

From 1970 to 1980, house prices went up from about $20,000 to about $60,000.

If you bought a house in 1970 with a 20% down payment (roughly $4,000), you'd be sitting on a 784% return on your initial investment a decade later. (This return doesn't include property taxes or interest or anything. It's just comparing the initial equity in 1970 – the down payment – to the rise in value by 1980.)

1970s HOUSING GAINS	
Starting price, January 1, 1970	$22,000
Ending price, December 31, 1979	$56,500
Down payment (starting capital)	$4,400
Capital gain	$34,500
Return on starting capital	784%

www.stansberryresearch.com

Here's the thing: Housing was affordable in the early 1970s. And house prices soared. In 2016 – after the great bust and with our ultra-low mortgage rates – housing is affordable again. Triple-digit gains – even with a big down payment like in the example above – are possible. I expect we'll see them!

I've been "pounding the table" on real estate in recent years. I hope you've followed my advice... You should be up at this point already. The good news is, it ain't over yet!

Remember, buying a house – specifically, by taking out a mortgage – is the perfect hedge against a weakening dollar. You're betting against the dollar and betting on your home – and housing in general.

Considering the direction our country is headed, and given the historic lows we now have in housing, this is the absolute best investment you can make over the next several years.

You haven't missed it yet... but the opportunity will go away eventually. Get on it while you can!

The Best Way to Legally Buy and Sell Gold I've Ever Seen

As of March 2016, there's a way you can buy gold at more than $80 off melt value.

It's the best way to buy gold I've ever seen.

This investment is also the best way to sell gold... because when you sell this investment, **you will NOT pay the usual taxes**.

Even better, chances are good that you will not only be able to buy gold at a discount to melt value, but you will be able to sell it at a premium as well.

Lastly, it's easy to do... This investment trades in the U.S., just like a stock.

It's the absolute best way to buy and sell gold.

This investment allows us to own silver at a discount, as well... with the same great tax benefits.

Simply put, if you're interested in owning precious metals, this is an investment you need to understand...

How You Can Buy Gold and Silver at a 7% Discount to Melt Value

In 1961, the **Central Fund of Canada (NYSE: CEF)** was born... and in 1983, it re-defined its mandate to become the "Sound Monetary Fund."

The Central Fund of Canada made a commitment to hold gold and silver... nothing else. Gold makes up 64% of the fund. Silver makes up 36%.

The fund primarily holds gold and silver bullion in a bank vault in Canada. It doesn't buy, sell, or trade. It simply sits on its precious metals in Canada. This is important to the Internal Revenue Service (IRS). It gives you a much better tax treatment when you sell the stock.

The Central Fund of Canada is big. Its market value is several billion dollars. Its expense ratio for 2015 was just 0.31%. For the full details on the fund, go to www.CentralFund.com.

The Central Fund of Canada organized itself as a closed-end fund, which means it has a fixed amount of shares outstanding. (This is different than an exchange-traded fund, or "ETF," which can create and liquidate shares based on demand.)

As a closed-end fund, the Central Fund of Canada also has a fixed amount of gold and silver that it sits on. It can't change how it owns these precious metals.

This gives us an opportunity to buy gold and silver at a discount as I write this in March 2016.

You see, when gold is "hot," investors pile into gold investments like this fund. And because the Central Fund of Canada has a fixed number of shares, increased demand forces it to trade for a premium greater than the melt value of its precious metals.

Gold was "hot" for more than a decade during the 2000s...

Since investors loved gold – and the security and simplicity of buying bullion in a Canadian vault through the stock market – the Central Fund of Canada traded for an average premium of 8% from 2002 to 2012.

But from 2011 through 2016, precious metals have been out of favor...

Investors haven't been interested in gold and silver. Sentiment has been so negative toward gold and silver that the Central Fund of Canada traded at a more than 7% discount to its liquidation value as of early 2016.

That's a remarkable change. And remember, the Central Fund of Canada only holds precious metals in bullion form in bank vaults in Canada. So you are buying gold and silver at a discount to melt value...

Since this fund trades on the U.S. stock market, it's the easiest way to buy bullion... You can buy and sell this fund every day without having to ship gold and silver around. You don't need to take delivery of your bullion or figure out where to store it.

And you can buy it at a 7% discount. At a $1,250-per-ounce gold price, that's like buying gold for roughly $87.50 below melt value.

I expect that when gold and silver get "hot" again, this fund will return to trading at a premium. **Remember, it traded for an average premium of 8% during the last gold bull market**.

There's also another big benefit here... *When it comes time to pay income taxes on this, you won't have to pay what you would normally pay for precious metals...*

Generally with precious metals investing, you pay a flat 28% "collectibles" tax. Most people don't know it – they get a nasty surprise at tax time – but that 28% collectibles tax even applies to precious metals ETFs, like the SPDR Gold Shares Fund (GLD).

However, in the case of the Central Fund of Canada, two unique features allow it to be taxed at your normal, long-term capital-gains rate (15% for most people):

1. It's based in Canada, so it's foreign.

2. It passively holds metals instead of trading them. So the IRS classifies this fund as a passive foreign investment company ("PFIC").

On the downside, this forces you to fill out an extra form at tax time. (You make the "QEF election" on that form – details are on the fund's website, www.CentralFund.com.) **But it's completely worth it... You're cutting your tax bill nearly in half – from the 28% collectibles tax rate to the 15% long-term capital-gains tax rate**.

In sum, the Central Fund of Canada is the absolute best way to buy and sell gold and silver. When you compare it with the common "easy" way to buy gold in the stock market – GLD – the decision is obvious. Just take a look at this comparison table...

THE BEST WAY TO BUY AND SELL GOLD		
	Central Fund of Canada (CEF)	SPDR Gold Shares Fund (GLD)
Tax Rate	15%*	28%
Discount	7%	0%
Expense Ratio	0.32%	0.40%

* 20% if you're in the 39.6% income bracket

www.stansberryresearch.com

Shares of the Central Fund of Canada win in every important criterion, hands down. It's a no-brainer.

This is the best way I've ever seen to invest in precious metals. You're buying gold and silver at a 7% discount to liquidation value through this fund.

It's big, with a multibillion-dollar market value. It's easy to trade on the New York Stock Exchange with the symbol CEF. And there's no need to worry about delivery or storage of physical bullion.

If you're interested in gold for the long term, I urge you to check out shares of the **Central Fund of Canada (NYSE: CEF)** – as long as you're buying at a discount of 5% or greater. (To see the discount, go to www.CentralFund.com, and then click on "Net Asset Value.")

Dr. Steve Sjuggerud's Top Ideas

- Before the crisis arrives, you need to get a huge portion of your wealth OUT of the U.S dollar... and INTO investments that will maintain and increase their value as the dollar declines.

  The two best ways to do this are investing in real estate and precious metals.

- Home prices and mortgage rates have gone up since the bottom in 2013. But you haven't missed the opportunity in real estate yet. 2016 is still an incredible time to buy and own property. The two secrets that will allow you to succeed in property are: 1) Don't get stuck on getting the lowest price, and 2) buy the good stuff now even though it has moved up in price.

- If you're interested in gold for the long term, buy shares of the **Central Fund of Canada (NYSE: CEF)** – as long as you are buying at a discount of 5% or greater. (To see the discount, go to www.CentralFund.com, and then click on "Net Asset Value.")

  To be the most tax-efficient with this fund, plan on holding for at least one year. Sell if the price rises to more than a 5% premium. Otherwise, consider it your primary way to hold gold and silver bullion.

LETTERS FROM

Dr. David Eifrig, Jr.

Before joining Stansberry Research in 2008, Dr. David "Doc" Eifrig, Jr. worked in arbitrage and trading groups with major Wall Street investment banks, including Goldman Sachs, Chase Manhattan, and Yamaichi in Japan. He is also a board-eligible ophthalmologist and has published peer-reviewed medical research.

At Stansberry Research, he shares his love for empowering people with his finance and medical knowledge...

Doc's largest monthly publication, *Retirement Millionaire,* shows 100,000-plus readers how to live a millionaire lifestyle on less money than you'd imagine possible. *Retirement Trader* shows readers a safe way to double or triple the gains in their retirement accounts with less risk. *Income Intelligence* shows investors how to analyze the income markets to maximize their income and total returns.

His free daily newsletter, *Retirement Millionaire Daily*, is filled with "hacks," ideas, secrets, and strategies that can save you money... save you time... or even save your life.

Doc has one of the best track records in the financial-newsletter business. From 2010 to 2013, he closed 136 winning positions in a row for his *Retirement Trader* subscribers.

He is also the author of four books: *The Doctor's Protocol Field Manual, High Income Retirement, The Living Cure,* and *Dr. David Eifrig's Big Book of Retirement Secrets.*

In the following essays, Doc suggests five steps to take control of your own retirement and keep your money out of the hands of corrupt mainstream institutions. He also details a health care plan in which you can build your savings tax-free – and even pass them on to your children.

Get Some Money off the Financial Grid

There's a seismic shift taking place in America right now... one you must absolutely pay attention to because it's going to dramatically affect your money.

I'm talking about the near-complete corruption of the mainstream institutions we've entrusted to handle our money... specifically, Wall Street firms and the big banks.

Most Americans are naïve about what's really happening with their money while inside these institutions. If you have a money market fund, for example, it's likely that some of your money has been placed into risky debt instruments. And you're likely being paid less than 0.1% for taking such big risks!

If you own regular stocks, your broker is probably borrowing shares from your account to execute *other* trades without your approval. It's completely legal. But most Americans have no idea this is going on.

Plus, as we've seen in case after case, when companies get in trouble (like MF Global), they are likely to "co-mingle" your money with their firm's to cover their mistake.

In short, the culture of our financial system is radically changing, and this trend is likely to accelerate in the coming years. Sure, people weren't complete angels when I worked on Wall Street. But there was at least a general respect for your customer and an interest in the well-being of your firm.

In 2016, it has become every man for himself.

We have cheating on every level... Banks are allowed to manipulate interest rates. Big, well-known companies "fudge" their numbers to inflate their earnings – basically lying to shareholders. I'm talking about supposed icons of American enterprise, companies like Time Warner, Xerox, Merck, Bristol-Myers, AIG Insurance, Merrill Lynch, Citigroup, and Rite Aid, just to name a few.

Many Wall Street stock analysts have lied about stocks they recommend to the public. Henry Blodgett of Merrill Lynch, for example, called stocks he was promoting to public investors "crap" and a "piece of junk" in private e-mails.

Even the government is in on the action...

In a closed-door meeting, held well BEFORE the big financial collapse, Henry Paulson, the U.S. Treasury secretary (and ex-Goldman Sachs boss of mine) apparently explained to around 20 hedge-fund managers and other top Wall Street executives that mortgage giants Fannie Mae and Freddie Mac would require huge, multibillion-dollar bailouts... the U.S. government would have to take over... and their shareholders would be completely wiped out.

And yet, in front of Congress, Paulson said exactly the opposite.

So you had a high-ranking government official, explicitly lying to Congress (and, by extension, the general public), while giving the real facts to a group of people who represented the financial interests of the world's wealthiest folks. Disgusting behavior.

Who picked up the tab?

We did, of course, and the rest of America's taxpayers.

Any way you look at it... it's clear that Wall Street and big banking has adopted a "get mine at any cost" mentality. There's absolutely no way to tell what crime these big institutions are going to commit with your money next.

So what can you do?

It's critical for you to get at least *some* of your money "off the financial grid" and beyond the grasp of the Wall Street "system."

It's easier to do than you may think. In this chapter, I'll show you the simple but necessary steps you can take to protect yourself...

Step No. 1: Take Control of Your Retirement Money

In 2012, Hostess Brands – the bankrupt baked-goods company – admitted to using workers' pensions to pay for company operations. Hostess misused retirement funds and missed more than $20 million in pension payments.

Don't trust your employer to do what's best for your retirement.

If you're more than 40 years old, you may have a "pension," also known as a defined benefits plan. It's a retirement account that your employer funds and controls. When you retire, your employer agrees to give you either a lump sum of money or monthly payments. To get a pension, you must meet basic eligibility requirements like working for the company for a minimum number of years.

With a pension, you have zero control over what happens. You can't increase or decrease the amount that's being invested. Companies also hire managers who oversee where pension money is invested, and the fees they charge dilute returns. Plus, if you die right after you retire, your dependents might get nothing.

But there is a solution... You can move money from your pension into a **self-directed IRA**. This gives you total control of your money. You get to grow your money tax-free just like a pension, but there's no limit on how much you can make.

A self-directed IRA is exactly what it sounds like... It puts you in charge of what you invest in. In addition to the conventional investments you can make in a typical IRA – like stocks, bonds, and options (something I regularly recommend to my *Retirement Trader* readers) – a fully self-directed IRA allows you to invest in many other assets, including real estate, private stocks, businesses, and even precious metals.

You can invest in just about anything, as long as it's not employed for your personal benefit. This simply means you must avoid any conflicts of interest. You can't, for example, invest in companies you have a 50% interest in. But you can buy the house next door through your IRA and then rent it to a neighbor. You can also invest in a local small business (again, as long as it's not your own).

I use my self-directed IRA to generate income by selling stock options. When I use this account for options trading, I don't have to follow any accounting or tax requirements.

In fact, if you do all your trading inside a retirement account, you don't have to report any trades to the IRS. The goal is simply to maximize your total returns as quickly and as easily as you can... And get better returns than a pension could offer.

There are two ways to move your pension to an IRA. One is to roll over the pension directly into an IRA. The broker or custodian you're opening an IRA with should have all the necessary forms for you to fill out. I have mine with Fidelity and TD Ameritrade.

You can also take a lump sum payment on your pension and then move the funds into an IRA. If you do this within days of taking the lump sum, you'll avoid being taxed on the money and the 10% early withdrawal penalty. If you can just roll over the pension directly, you don't risk incurring taxes and penalties.

Step No. 2: Put Your Money in a 'Safety Bank'

Holding cash helps many of us sleep well at night. We get peace of mind knowing we won't lose money. But leaving money in a traditional savings account earns little or no interest.

I've uncovered a safe way to earn more on our cash. We can also lower our risks, help local communities, and turn our noses up at the big money-centric banks that are sucking our lifeblood.

Here's what I want you to do: **Join a credit union**.

You've probably heard of a credit union. But if you're like most folks I've talked with, you figure there's no real practical difference between a credit union and a big-name bank. But they are different. And at times like this, the benefits of joining a credit union are important.

Simply put, credit unions are nonprofit companies that act as local community banks. And guess what? Credit unions offer much better rates than what you'll find at a bank.

In 2016, a bank might offer 0.27% on one-year certificates of deposit... but you could make 0.51% at a credit union. Say you put $20,000 into an account. You'd make $54 in the first year with the bank, but $102 in the first year in the credit union.

The best part is, Wall Street doesn't have access to that money anymore.

You see, the credit union turns around and loans your money to other members. Rather than investing in insider shell games like mortgage-backed securities, the credit union's bread and butter is making auto, boat, and housing loans to the local community.

Unlike Wall Street, the board members meet locally in a credit union conference room, not on some island resort spending shareholders' money. Even better, the board members are usually volunteers.

Are there any risks? Not really. Your money is as safe, if not safer than the larger commercial banks. Just like the Federal Deposit Insurance Corp. ("FDIC"), which is supposed to insure your deposits in a commercial bank, credit unions have the National Credit Union Share Insurance Fund ("NCUSIF"). This fund is backed by the "full faith and credit of the United States government," too. Just like commercial banks, each individual is insured up to $250,000.

The only catch is to join a credit union, you are legally required to have some sort of affiliation with the group that sponsors it. For some credit unions, you have to work for particular employers. But in other cases, you need only be a resident of a particular state. In my case, my dad was a state employee in North Carolina, which qualified me to join.

By banking with a local credit union, you're giving your capital to local people and businesses instead of the huge Wall Street firms that often use it to pay their executives big, fat bonuses.

Keep your money local. You'll support small and local business ventures near you. I don't know about you, but I don't want to pay for any more golf trips, big bonuses, or million-dollar office decorations.

To find out more about how to join a credit union, go to www. asmarterchoice.org.

Step No. 3: An 'Insurance Currency' Created by the U.S. Government

This step involves quietly moving some of your money into a particular type of U.S. government-created "insurance currency," as I call it.

You can own U.S. currency that looks just like regular currency... but is totally protected from a decline in the U.S. dollar. Your money will be safer, in case there are problems in the financial system.

I'm talking about **silver**.

Silver has been used as money for longer and in more parts of the world than gold. The words for "silver" and "money" are identical in 51 countries. The bottom line is that silver was money long before the existence of paper and electronic currencies.

Today, with U.S. government spending out of control and debt exploding, silver could be the sort of metal that countries turn to as a store of value and backing for their currencies.

Silver is an easier and simpler metal than gold to use as money. If all hell breaks loose and China or crazy U.S. politicians debase the dollar, silver will be the better choice for transactions. After all, a one-ounce silver coin is worth about $15. That matches up well with common prices of everyday goods.

Imagine trying to pay for an oil change... Wouldn't it be easier to hand the mechanic a couple silver dollars than to borrow his metal cutters to shave off 2% of a $1,000 gold Krugerrand coin?

Silver is simply more practical.

You have a lot of ways to invest in silver. But the best way I've found allows you to take physical possession of the metal without paying huge markups to the spot price (like you would buying rare coins). It doesn't require risky leverage or buying of mining companies that may or may not be around this time next year.

Instead, you can own real, hold-in-your-hand silver for less than $3.

The opportunity to own this type of silver began more than 200 years ago, when Congress designated silver as the material for the first American coin. Congress based its new dollar on the Spanish piaster, though it took its name from a German coin called the thaler.

President Lyndon B. Johnson signed the Coinage Act of 1965 to eliminate most of the silver from coins. Half dollars changed from 90% silver to 40% silver... while dimes and quarters changed to no silver (75% copper and 25% nickel).

Five years later, Congress pulled the remaining silver from the coins.

Today, coins dated before 1965 are known as "junk silver." They get tagged as "junk" because they have no value to collectors. They circulated widely in pockets and purses and show a lot of wear. By one estimate, more than 13 billion of these coins are spread around the country.

But that's great for us as investors.

Because they don't have collectible value, these coins can be purchased right now at just $0.50 per ounce more than silver's current spot-market price. That's significant since collectible and uncirculated silver coins often have premiums of 25%-50% more than the spot price. (The 2011 $1 Silver Eagle, for example, sells for *nearly five times* the price of silver). So junk silver gives us an immediate 25%-30% discount to other types of silver coins.

How do you buy it? Junk silver comes in $1,000 face-value bags of dimes, quarters, or half dollars. So the breakdown of a bag could be any of the following three...

- 10,000 dimes

- 4,000 quarters

- 2,000 half dollars

Regardless of which denomination you choose, the amount of silver you buy is the same... about 715-720 ounces.

Right now, the current retail price for a $1,000 face-value bag of junk silver is about $14,000 plus shipping and insurance (which varies depending upon the delivery location, usually ranging from $60-$120).

So let's say the total cost is about $14,100. Divide that by 10,000 dimes and you get real, hold-in-your-hand silver for just $1.41. (Keep in mind, this value can fluctuate daily with the price of silver and with demand.) And that's why we say you can get silver for less than $3.

Growing demand will push up dealer premiums on junk silver, further multiplying your gains.

But remember, silver is volatile. Any change in the price of silver could change your total cost. For the most current price, you can call a reputable dealer...

Buying silver and gold can be risky business if you don't know whom you are dealing with. Over the years, we at Stansberry Research have formed some reliable contacts in all areas of the financial world. Here are a few reputable folks who "hoard" coins. Feel free to tell them we sent you...

Van Simmons
David Hall Rare Coins
P.O. Box 6220
Newport Beach, CA 92658
Phone: 800-759-7575 or 949-567-1325
E-mail: info@davidhall.com

Rich Checkan
Asset Strategies International
1700 Rockville Pike, Suite 400
Rockville, MD 20852
Phone: 800-831-0007 or 301-881-8600
Fax: 301-881-1936
E-mail: rcheckan@assetstrategies.com

Parker Vogt
Camino Coin 1301 Broadway Ave.
Burlingame, CA 94010
Phone: 800-348-8001 or 650-348-3000
E-mail: Parker@caminocompany.com

Rest assured, we receive no compensation for mentioning them. We just know they treat our readers well.

You can always check the live price of silver at: www.kitco.com.

Step No. 4: Protect Your Investments from a Stock Market Crisis

Years ago, before online trading become popular, companies used to issue **paper stock certificates**. The certificates typically included the number of shares owned, the date, a corporate seal, signatures from company officers, and your information. It represented your personal ownership of a piece of a company.

But over the years, this became more costly than brokers keeping electronic records. If you're investing with a broker, it's likely the shares are in the brokerage's name not yours. This practice is called "street name" registration. The "street name" is the name of the broker... who keeps an electronic form of the stock certificate.

There are a couple reasons this practice is common. First, it's convenient. Your broker can quickly complete transactions electronically without you having to mail money to a company and wait weeks to get a paper certificate.

Second, the broker holding electronic records of the stock purchase reduces the risk of theft, loss, or physical damage.

Unfortunately, for average investors like us, this lets brokers use our money however they want to. A broker can use your money for speculative trades and even loan your shares to short sellers – which could drive down the value of your shares.

If a brokerage firm goes bankrupt, it can use your shares as assets to pay off its creditors unless the shares are in your name. We've already seen it happen.

In 2011, MF Global – a financial derivatives broker – filed for Chapter 11 bankruptcy. MF Global had been using customers' funds to cover trading losses. Some estimates show MF Global customers lost $1.6 billion, most of which has yet to be returned.

But there are two ways to protect yourself and get stock in your name: paper certificates and direct registration.

Whether you buy shares directly from a company or through your broker, you can request a physical paper certificate be sent to you. There could be a fee for this, but you'll get the paper certificate in your name and any company information will be sent directly to you rather than relying on your broker to send it.

The downside is that if you lose your certificate, it can be hard to prove you owned it. And there's usually a charge to replace a certificate. Also, if you decide it's time to sell, it takes longer than using a broker's platform.

The other method is through direct registration. You can request your broker to handle direct registration (if the company you want to invest in offers it). Buying shares from the company and skipping your broker is another way to get direct registration. You won't get a certificate, as the company is holding the shares, but you'll be listed as owner of the shares.

Like paper certificates, purchases and sales are slower if you buy directly from the company. Another problem you might encounter is that not all companies allow for direct registration. You can contact your broker to find out which of the companies that you're interest in offer this option.

Step No. 5: Make Some of Your Money 'Invisible'

There's a legal way to keep some of your money hidden from the government...

Invest in **a specific group of rare gold coins**.

In 1904, Teddy Roosevelt commissioned Augustus Saint-Gaudens (the foremost sculptor of the day) to create a coin to reflect America's status as the most powerful nation on Earth.

Though in poor health, Saint-Gaudens delivered. He designed the gallant $20 "Double Eagle" gold piece, a design that today is considered the most beautiful coin of all time. It was Saint-Gaudens' last work. He died and never saw the fruits of his labor.

The coins were minted from 1907 until 1933. After gold ownership was banned in 1933, private ownership of gold was not allowed in the U.S. until 1974.

In early 2016, a Saint-Gaudens $20 gold piece would have an intrinsic value of about $1,200, since it contains nearly an ounce of gold, and an ounce of gold is worth about $1,200. Yet its value is much higher.

Of course, coin enthusiasts will always pay more than "meltdown value" for Saint-Gaudens $20 gold pieces (since they're considered to be the most beautiful coins in the world). But you can own a piece of history, and own real money with real gold, for a small premium over the meltdown value.

The $20 Saint-Gaudens is one of the world's most famous coins. The coin was difficult to mint as it has high-relief designs, which were problematic for production.

The coin didn't see a lot of circulation at the time of issue. It was used mostly for international trade and interbank payments. Consequently, most survivors are in lower-grade uncirculated condition (known as "Commercial Uncs" in the trade).

Saint-Gaudens coins minted from 1924 to 1928, for example, have a high collectible value, yet they are easy to buy and sell. Like bullion coins, there are enough of them to go around, plus they contain a little less than an ounce of gold (0.87 of an ounce). Depending on the vintages, the coins are in good supply – coin dealers use the term "common dates" for those. Common dates include 1904, 1908, and 1924.

When buying these coins, you should consider the vintage rarity and the condition of the coin as graded by a professional grading service. I'd recommend sticking with coins with mint states (MS) between MS-63 and MS-65. (For more on this grading system, read Van Simmons' interview starting on page 168.) Coins with higher mint states have few blemishes. As such, they have more collectible value.

Graded coins are packed in a sealed plastic holder meant to protect and authenticate the coin. So be sure you buy this sort of coin. It's usually easiest to do so from reputable sellers.

One of the keys to buying these hybrid coins is to buy them when the ratio to gold bullion prices is low. Right now, the MS-65 Saint-Gaudens coins are trading at a 48% premium to gold. This is one of the lowest valuations in the last 50 years. Lower-rated coins like the MS-63 trade at just 25% premiums to bullion value. This is also one of the lowest prices relative to gold in history.

To take advantage of this low premium opportunity, I recommend you buy the **MS-65 Saint-Gaudens**. The MS-65s traded at 800% over the melt value of gold back in 1986, when gold had its extreme run up. If this sort of premium were to return, or even half that, you could easily make 35%-45% on these collector classics.

I wouldn't put more than 5% of your investment in coins like these, or any investment category.

As with silver, you can always check the live price of gold at: www.kitco.com.

How to Instantly Increase the Power of Your Retirement Savings by 200%

It's the most fascinating financial product I've ever seen.

I was investing my college money more than 30 years ago. I spent years with trading geniuses at Goldman Sachs. I lived in the world's three biggest financial hubs. And now that I work for one of the world's largest financial publishers, I'm surrounded by new investment ideas every single day.

Several years ago, in Florida, I found the most fascinating financial product I've ever seen. It has to be... because it addresses the biggest fear every American has: That late in life, our health will fail and we'll run out of money, ending up sick and destitute.

Just consider: Medicare reports 30% of all health care dollars are spent in the last 12 months of life. And 401(k) behemoth Fidelity Investments reports 65-year-olds will need $240,000 for health care before they die.

Please don't count on Obama or Washington to pay your bills and hold your hand while you die. Medicare doesn't cover everything you'll need (long-term care, for instance).

And worse, it lowers your chances to die with dignity.

Bureaucrats are worried about budgets, not your quality of life... And they aren't any good at managing budgets, so payouts and benefits rarely match patient needs. Most of us are going to need a pile of cash or the ability to easily tap assets to make ends meet. How much probably depends on your health and family history.

If you already have a little cash for emergencies – and you should – I've found a way to at least triple the value of your cash overnight.

This product will allow you to safely move rainy-day money from one type of savings to another and guarantee the care and comfort you want should your health turn sour. And if you remain healthy until passing, you still keep your savings (and can pass them on to your children) – *not give them to the government.*

Annuities and Long-Term Care

The investment I'm talking about is an Asset-Based Care (ABC). Despite its relative newness – this insurance product didn't exist before November 1, 2009 – an ABC is safe, liquid, and yields more than most certificates of deposit (CDs) at your local bank.

Essentially, an ABC is an annuity on steroids.

You can find all kinds of annuities on the market. But in essence, they are insurance products that guarantee income for a holder's lifetime (or periods like five or 10 years).

For example, I could pay $10,000 at age 50 in exchange for a payment of $50 a month until I die. If I lived to 80, I'd receive $18,000 (30 years x 12 months per year x $50) from that initial $10,000.

However, the details vary. You can buy annuities with a single, lump-sum payment or extend your principal across multiple payments. Annuities can pay at fixed or variable rates, and you can opt for deferred or immediate payouts.

As I said at the outset, Medicare doesn't pay for long-term care like nursing homes. You have to use up your personal assets and declare yourself broke before Medicaid will cover it... Even then, not all costs are covered. Worse, statistics say about 50% of us will need nursing home care at some point in our lives. And it's not cheap. A nursing home can cost about $91,000 a year. In-home care can run $45,000 a year.

Insurance companies offer policies designed to cover these costs.
But conventional policies are expensive, and the application process
is burdensome. For example, a 70-year-old male might pay close to
$3,000 a year for $4,000-a-month of benefits. And the benefits last
for only three years, which adds up to only $144,000 of benefits. And
that's if you can actually get insured at age 70. Most policies require
full underwriting, including physicals, blood tests, etc.

And remember, there's only a 50-50 chance you'll even use that
policy. It's a coin flip. You could easily spend $60,000 of your
money for nothing except a little peace of mind. If you don't go to a
nursing home (or similar facility), the insurance company keeps your
premium. It's a "use it or lose it" proposition.

But ABCs are different. You keep everything.

How to Leverage Your Cash Safely

The ABCs combine annuities with long-term-care insurance. Here's
what you get...

1. Long-term tax-deferred growth of savings

2. Long-term care benefits

3. A meteoric increase in the value of your benefits

4. Retain all money if you don't use the long-term care (LTC) benefit

5. The ability to pass on the money to your heirs

Here's how ABCs work: Imagine you're 70 years old and have
$100,000 in four different certificates of deposit (CDs) with credit
unions all earning 0.5% to 1.5%. The CDs are simply contracts that pay
a fixed amount of interest over an agreed-upon term. You pay taxes on
the interest, and your heirs get the money on your passing.

If you needed to go to a nursing home, your money would dry up in 13 months (26 months if you could use in-home care). Then you'd have to tap the rest of your assets. If you outlive those assets, your family would pay for the rest of your care (and decide your fate since they control the purse strings).

Instead, if you bought an ABC plan with that $100,000, the insurance company places it in an account with an interest rate around 2.65% to 3%. Your money grows tax-deferred... but you also get long-term care insurance. A small percentage of your account balance pays the insurance.

Your Cash Explodes in Value

At the end of one year, your annuity's accumulated value becomes $100,612. But should you actually need to tap that value for long-term care, the total-care benefit explodes to $301,835.

You can tap into that total-care benefit the moment you are unable to perform your daily living – formally called "activities of daily living." I'll tell you exactly what that means in a moment.

In this case, you'd get $4,192 a month for up to six years (total payments: $301,835). Again, that's from an initial deposit of only $100,000. This is a true tripling of your savings or assets into protection for long-term care. It's as if you earned 50% a year on your initial investment for six years.

If you don't ever use long-term care, your initial deposit is still earning tax-deferred interest. It's not a "use it or lose it" deal. In fact, you're free to use the $100,000 at any time.

To top it all off: **The money you receive from these policies is tax-free**. Yep, not just *tax-deferred* but actually 100% *tax-free* at the federal and state level. This is a true win-win deal.

Here's a way to shift money from one form of savings (money markets and CDs) and put it into another (an ABC plan) and make your net worth explode in value and grow tax-deferred and tax-free. I can't imagine Congress letting this deal stand on the books for long.

Thanks to a provision in the Pension Protection Act of 2006, effective January 1, 2010, you can make a *1035 exchange* and transfer an old annuity into an ABC annuity. Any tax-deferred gains from your old annuity can be withdrawn 100% tax-free in your ABC annuity as long as the withdrawals are used to cover long-term care related expenses.

The Risks Are Covered

Of course, with any investment, ABCs come with some risk. But it's the same risk you take any time you buy insurance... Does the company have the ability to pay the claims?

First, in the case of ABC plans, companies are required by state law to keep cash and securities liquid to pay benefits on their policies. Thus, the risk with companies in this business is low.

Second, you can check out the claims-paying abilities of any insurance company by looking at ratings provided by either Standard & Poor's or A.M. Best.

What to Do Next...

If this sort of policy makes sense to you and you have a pile of savings for a rainy day, I urge you to look into setting up an ABC, especially if you sense you'll eventually need long-term care.

Qualifying is easy if you're healthy. The application can be done and approved over the phone, unlike the regular LTC plans that require a full underwriting process.

Only a handful of national insurance companies offer them – Genworth and Nationwide among them.

One option to investigate is the Indiana-based insurance company

Forethought Life. Forethought is A-rated with A.M. Best and Standard & Poor's and B-rated with Weiss. Forethought Life's ForeCare Annuity offers one of the better "explosions" of your asset value out there. Your money is safe with companies rated so highly.

Alternately, I recommend giving a father-son team I trust a call – David and Todd Phillips of Estate Planning Specialists LLC. They specialize in the estate and long-term care planning business. Feel free to tell them we sent you... and let us know how it goes... 888-892-1102 or e-mail them at david@epmez.com or todd@epmez.com. (I have no financial connection.)

Dr. David Eifrig's Top Ideas

- Two ways to take control of your own retirement funds and keep it out of the hands of the government are to join a credit union instead of a big-name bank and to create a self-directed IRA.

  Dr. Eifrig uses his self-directed IRA to generate income by selling stock options. When this account is used for options trading, you don't have to follow standard accounting and tax requirements.

- Doc recommends asset-based care (ABC) as a way to at least triple the value of your cash overnight. Your initial deposit still earns tax-deferred interest. So the money you receive from these policies is tax-free. It's not just tax-deferred; it's actually 100% tax-free at the federal and state level. This is a true win-win deal.

LETTERS FROM

Van Simmons

A consummate collector and dedicated numismatist, Van Simmons has earned his place in the rare coin pantheon as the leading coin merchant of his time. He specializes in portfolio construction, set building, and helping clients acquire the world's finest rare coins.

Van has been a rare-coin collector since age 12 and a rare-coin dealer since 1979. As one of the founders of Professional Coin Grading Service (PCGS), the largest rare-coin grading service in the world, he has helped revolutionize the rare-coin market. PCGS has graded and certified more than 31 million coins in the last 30 years. PCGS has more than 1,300 authorized dealers worldwide.

Van is also the president of David Hall Rare Coins and the co-founder of Collectors Universe (CLCT), a publically traded company on the Nasdaq Exchange. He holds a seat on the Board of Directors, and he holds a certificate of "Advanced Professional Director" with the Corporate Directors Group.

In the following interview, Van discusses how collectables hold up against bear markets and economic depressions. He also identifies which alternative investments – including the single-most undervalued collectables asset class – are the smartest choices to legally hide your money from the government.

An Alternative Market That Will Hide Your Cash From the Government

Sean Goldsmith: Van, everybody's portfolio is getting whacked right now, but you said that your collectables are holding up well. Could you talk about how they're not really correlated with the stock market, and what you're seeing in the collectibles market compared to the stock market?

Van Simmons: Sure. If the stock market goes down, the economy loses trillions of dollars. If it falls too much, it will affect everything – including collectibles. But most of the stock market selloffs that I've seen in the last 20 years haven't affected the coin market or most other collectables markets at all. In some cases, certain markets may slow down for a while.

Most collectables markets are smaller than the coin market. The antique gun market is small, for example, and the buyers are passionate. The same is true for Tiffany lamps. These types of collectables markets tend to hold up well regardless of market condition.

The coin market is probably 10 to 20 times larger than most other collectable asset classes. It may get a little volatile from time to time. In the last several years, the only area of the coin market that has taken a big hit is generic gold coins, which have tracked gold's falling price over the past three years.

But rare gold coins – those that are older, scarcer, and higher-grade – have remained extremely strong.

A good example is the early Proof Gold issues from 1858 to 1880. A proof $20 Liberty is a rare coin in high grades. I sold two of them for a client, one being an early 1860s (Civil War era) coin in a high grade. Five years ago, the coin would have sold in the $200k range. It sold in 2015 for more than $500k.

Coins struck throughout the 1800s (including $0.03 silver pieces, barber quarters, dimes, liberty-seated dimes, and half dollars) have been the cornerstone of the market for the last 100 years. They've been solid over the last five or 10 years.

Prices for these different coins have gone both up and down. But 1800s coins are one of the least-expensive areas of the rare coin market. If you looked at my personal portfolio, I'd estimate 65%-70% of my coin portfolio is invested in these 19th-century type coins.

If you break down my investment strategy in the gold market, I put approximately 25% of my allocation into gold bullion, 25% into gold stocks, and 50% into rare coins. I diversify into those three areas. And I think all three are reasonably priced in 2016.

Goldsmith: What are some of the best values that you're seeing in rare coins where premiums have collapsed? Or just some great deals we may not see for the next decade or two?

Simmons: One of the coins that has always been promoted heavily (because it's popular and available) is a $20 Saint-Gaudens Grade MS-65. People buy and sell these in quantity every day. Saint-Gaudens were struck from 1907 to 1933.

There are 11 grades of MS-65 uncirculated coins. The company I co-founded 30 years ago – Professional Coin Grading Service (PCGS) – has graded probably 31 million coins since we started. Of those, we've graded a little more than 130,000 MS-65 Saint-Gaudens, which sell for about $1,700 each today.

Another popular coin is the $20 Liberty gold piece. These were struck from 1849 to 1907. Unlike the Saint-Gaudens, which were usually uncirculated, Liberties were usually spent. After the turn of the 20th century, people started saving $20 gold pieces and carrying paper money. So most of the Saint-Gaudens were saved.

$20 Liberties were made for a longer period of time than Saint-Gaudens, but we've graded much fewer of them – only about 6,100 $20 Liberties in MS-65.

So even though $20 Liberties are about 22 times rarer than Saint-Gaudens, they only sell for about $3,200 – not even double the price of Saint-Gaudens. They're the same-sized coin, but a $20 Liberty is a much better value than a Saint-Gaudens.

Another laughably cheap coin is the $10 Liberty. Most of them are dated 1901 at MS-65. And they sell for around $3,200. We've probably only graded 1,650 of those over the last 30 years, which makes them 70 times rarer than MS-65 Saint-Gaudens. But they've been overlooked, and the premiums have come way down in the last couple years.

Goldsmith: Do those coins ever trade at a premium in line with their rarity? What are some of the largest premiums you've seen on those two coins?

Simmons: Well, back in 1989-1990, when gold was around $400 an ounce, both of those coins were priced between $18,000 and $18,500.

Goldsmith: Wow. And they're trading for about $3,200 today, even though gold prices are nearly five times higher.

Simmons: Right. When one of the all-time classic, highly-collectable U.S. gold coins is trading for less than 20% of its previous high... It's worth taking a look.

Two other coins to consider today are the $2.50 Liberties and $5 Liberties Grade MS-65. Those coins are just free in my mind. The $2.50 Liberty sells in the $1,200 range and the $5 Liberty sells in the $3,000 range.

Goldsmith: So talk to me about silver. Do you think it's attractive right now?

Simmons: Everybody talks about the ratio of silver to gold. Historically, it was 16-to-1. Today, it's 79-to-1. That means one ounce of gold equals 79 ounces of silver.

I don't know if the ratio will ever revert to its historical average. People have been talking about the ratio for 30 years, but I don't know if we'll ever see that ratio again.

Also, it depends on whether you're speculating in metals to make money or you're investing in them to protect yourself against currency debasement and civil unrest.

Silver is an industrial metal. Its price fluctuates largely based on supply and demand. Based on all the studies I've seen, we mine less silver every year than we use (and I don't see any big supplies popping up). Still, if the economy slows down, silver could weaken.

Gold, on the other hand, is considered a global currency. The central banks of China, Russia, and the rest of the world own tons of gold. But none of them list one ounce of silver on their books – at least not any place I've been able to find it.

Another thing to consider... If you buy $10,000 worth of silver, you have 50 pounds. If you buy $10,000 worth of gold, you have a few ounces. Gold is more condensed and portable.

So I prefer to protect myself against a collapse of the dollar or the economy with gold. A lot of people will disagree and say you'll need silver to spend if a true crisis breaks out. That's true...

But I bought a ton of silver throughout the 1970s and 1980s. When I went to sell it, I had to load up my Volkswagen and about beat myself to death carrying these bags of silver that I bought for next to nothing. At that point, I told myself I'd never buy silver again just because of the hassle when you try to sell it.

Goldsmith: On the topic of gold's portability, I remember you telling me a story about your business partner, David Hall of David Hall Rare

Coins, pitching rare coins to a group of Chinese businessmen. Could you share that story again?

Simmons: As you know, there's a lot of money in China – several billionaires. A lawyer friend of ours came to my business partner and said he had some investors he wanted David to meet with.

So David went to China and presented to a room with 25 to 50 Chinese businessmen. They all sat stoic while he gave the rare-coin presentation (all through an interpreter).

As the meeting went on, David wasn't gaining traction. He showed a picture of an 1804 silver dollar that just sold for $5 million at auction. Then he showed a picture of a 1913 Liberty nickel that sold for $5.5 million at auction. Then he showed a 1794 silver dollar that sold for $9 million or $10 million at auction.

Finally, David pulled out five coins in PCGS holders, put them in his pocket, and said, "I'm leaving the country with $25 million." When the interpreter relayed that, the room lit up.

It turns out, the Chinese are looking for a way to get money out of the country. And coins are a great vehicle to transfer wealth from one country to another.

Goldsmith: I'm not sure if you're familiar with what's happening in the high-end real estate market right now... But in capital cities around the world, especially New York and Miami, the Chinese and other foreigners are buying hugely-expensive properties – the $100 million penthouses you hear about. They're buying them anonymously through holding companies because they're trying to quietly get cash out of their home country.

But the U.S. government announced it's cracking down on these anonymous purchases. So if the spigot into high-end real estate gets shut off, will that be a huge catalyst for rare coins?

Simmons: Certainly. That money will flow into all collectable areas the Chinese find interesting.

There's this new term for a class of tangible assets called "endurables." People are trying to buy things they can easily hide... So nobody knows where they are.

We saw a wealth tax in Cyprus, when the country was having financial problems. The government confiscated money from people's bank accounts. In the U.S., we have a wealth tax. It is called property tax... If you own a home, the government taxes you on it every year. If you don't pay it, they come and take it.

At some point, we'll probably see a wealth tax on bank accounts, brokerage accounts, retirement accounts, and everything else.

These endurable products – like rare coins – just "disappear"... and the government can't find them.

Goldsmith: Let's move out of the world of coins and on to the other collectables you're familiar with, like art and guns. What do you think is the single-most undervalued area right now?

Simmons: The gun market's reasonable. As I said, the collectors are very passionate.

Specifically, I'm talking about antique firearms, high-grade shotguns and things like that (not assault weapons). That market is underpriced for what you get. You can get a lot more for your money in guns right now than in a lot of other asset classes.

Another market that is underpriced is the San Francisco rock and roll posters from the 1960s, '70s, and early '80s. For $5,000 to $15,000, you can get world-class pieces.

At some point, you'll get really rich people that want an old Grateful Dead poster for their wall... To them, there's no difference between paying $15,000 or $25,000 for that poster.

For rock posters, I focus mostly on Rick Griffin. He's the icon for the whole industry. He's also a great story... He died in a motorcycle accident. He used to write comics for *Surfer Magazine*. Apparently, there's a movie in the works about his life story. I just think the focus over the next decade will be on him and his art. His is a classic story not unlike other artists who died early on and are now recognized as titans or icons in their field.

Goldsmith: So let's focus on rock posters. Tell me about the AOXOMOXOA Grateful Dead Poster by Rick Griffin.

Simmons: The poster was for a Dead concert in Hawaii. But the show got cancelled, so the posters were never released. In the industry, the rumor is there are only 30 to 35 of them that exist.

I was talking about this poster with the guy who used to manage Rick Griffin. I mentioned that there were 30 to 35 of these posters in existence. And he said, "No, there are 17."

I asked how he knew that... He told me he was there the day Rick picked them up. He took 17 of them home and threw the rest out. His manager claims Rick *threw them out*.

So how many are out there? There might be 15 today. They pop up at auction every once in a while. But most are damaged with tack holes. Posters are like all other collectables. You want to buy the highest quality you can.

I think that poster probably exists somewhere in mint condition. I've never seen one. I know it exists in near-mint because I own one.

My son and I travel to the San Francisco rock concert poster show every couple years. I was standing out front at 8 a.m. before the doors opened and there were several guys in their 70s and 80s standing in front of me waiting to get in. I found it interesting that several of these guys were smoking pot. I guess they were reliving their rock concert days.

Goldsmith: But it's not just the old guys listening to the Grateful Dead. My kids will listen to The Dead and their kids will listen to The Dead and other artists like Led Zeppelin and Jimi Hendrix. They're not going away.

Simmons: No.

Goldsmith: So the demand for those posters is going to be multigenerational. And if there's only 15 of the most highly collected poster, prices could go through the roof.

Simmons: I remember when I bought my first one. I think I paid $11,000 for it. The guy I bought it from asked me how much I thought the poster could be worth. I told him that if the market goes where I think it's going to go, it could be worth $100,000.

Now, a few years later, it's probably a $20,000 poster. In an area like this, you can see a lot of pressure squeezing prices so high because supply is so limited and popularity is so large.

Like you said... Your kids will listen to the Grateful Dead. Their music wasn't that great, but that's OK. I know you disagree with me on that, Sean...

But everybody still listens to Frank Sinatra. Everybody still listens to Elvis and, like you said, Jimi Hendrix. They won't be forgotten 20 or 30 years from now. They'll be as big or bigger than they are now because their music is so iconic. The popularity of the history of them is going to increase.

Goldsmith: Let's discuss another collectible – sports cards. Do you think those will have lasting value? My kids may listen to The Dead, but will they care about Ken Griffey, Jr.?

Simmons: You have the great icons of sports like Lou Gehrig, Babe Ruth, and Mickey Mantle, for example. Those icons will always be popular.

But in the baseball card market, you have to be selective. You either go with the great icons of the game, or you go with people that are going to be great in your generation. You buy them cheap when you can buy them cheap. And when the market runs up in five or 10 or 15 years, you sell them into the fever... Unless you just love them and want to hold them forever. But that's a whole different story.

Goldsmith: I'm sure you have some good war stories from collecting sports cards...

Simmons: In the early '80s, David and I opened the first real baseball card company for rare baseball cards. It was called American Card Exchange. We introduced a bid/ask market for cards. We'd say, "Here's what we'll pay for this card. Here's what we'll sell it for."

I was buying 1952 Topps Mickey Mantles for $1,000 to $1,500 a card. And they were classified as mint. Our current card company, Professional Sports Authenticator (PSA), grades them on a scale of one to 10.

So let's say the Mickey Mantle's I bought would grade between a seven and nine in today's market place. A nine just sold for nearly $1 million.

Goldsmith: Wow.

Simmons: I sold my Mickey Mantle in 1987 or 1988 for around $7,000 to $9,000, and thought I was getting rich. A few months ago, the same card – graded an eight – sold for $435,000. One of the heads of PSA told me a 10 would be worth about $5 million right now. So at $5 million, you have to really like Mickey Mantle.

Goldsmith: Clearly you know more about everything in collectables than I do. But I would argue that when you get to Mickey Mantle rookie cards or Picasso or Andy Warhol – that tier, the pinnacle of any market – it transcends that market and just becomes one of the most cherished assets in the world.

Simmons: True. I agree with that. Most assets in that category are fully priced until we have another big downturn. If we get some inflation, a lot of those expensive products will take off again. But some of them have gone up so much that it's becoming frightening.

A lot of people are looking for value. They just want to buy tangible assets that store value.

Some people say collectables will become worthless if we have a depression or major deflation.

Thirty years ago, I had a German doctor and his friend in my office. The friend asked that question – how do collectables perform during a depression? I told him, "I don't know. I've never lived through a depression."

And the German guy says, "No, you're wrong." He explained how his father supported a family of 10 people for six years following the first World War with his rare coin and rare stamp collection.

There's always somebody wealthy in the world who is willing to pay whatever it takes to get something for their collection – even during a depression.

When the German economy was melting down, inflation was so bad, they had billion Mark notes. Things were falling apart, but this German man's father was still able to sell his collectables for real money.

In 2008, in the midst of the subprime crisis, nobody knew if Merrill Lynch and Lehman Brothers were going to open the next day. You didn't know where interest rates were. You didn't know anything.

But during that period, I had three billionaire clients call in one week and asked if anyone was selling any great coins or great collectables. They were buying.

I remember telling one client, "Well, things haven't come down in price. Nobody's selling their coins." He told me price is not the object. He would pay whatever price necessary to get great stuff. He was looking for large diamonds, great art, great coins. He just wanted to put his money in something that he knew would have value 10-20 years down the road, regardless of the currency of the realm.

So what this German guy told me 30 years ago, I saw firsthand in 2008.

That's a good insurance policy.

Goldsmith: So backing up for a minute, the contemporary art market has gone totally insane. Paintings and sculptures are trading at more than $150 million. Do you think that's just a complete bubble?

Simmons: All markets go into complete bubbles and nobody knows how high they're going to go. I figure the higher they go, the farther they have to fall.

There was a six-foot tall Alberto Giacometti sculpture called the Walking Man. It was made in the 1960s and sold at auction for $105 million in 2010. Another Giacometti sculpture, Pointing Man, sold for $141 million last year. I don't get that at all.

I'm not saying they aren't worth the price... because that's what they sold for. And you can get two or three really rich guys to bid these prices up. But prices in that market may have been over-manipulated. Art dealers can be the best in the world at manipulating prices. That's their job for their clients. Nothing against them... They're great marketing people.

Art collectors are also super-passionate. So if somebody's collecting because they're passionate, they're great. Now there's a lot of foreign money just buying these artworks like assets.

But there are lots of other areas in the art market that are extremely undervalued and overlooked.

Goldsmith: Like what?

Simmons: There's an area called "scene paintings." In California, we have landscape artwork and things like plein-air art. These are outdoor paintings of fields and mountains. Collectors ran these prices to the moon, but they've come back down.

I recently bought a painting for $4,500 at auction. The woman who owned it paid $25,000 for it, then put a $4,000 frame on it.

I've personally purchased many California scene paintings, both oil paintings and watercolors.

These are basically paintings of America being built from the 1930s through the 1970s. I have a painting of a guy selling fruit with his family and his dog on the Pacific Coast Highway from the 1940s. I have paintings of people sitting on a bus bench and somebody working on a truck outside his house. These are scenes of daily life. They show what life was like during that period of time.

I focus on California scene paintings. But that's not the only area. You can buy great pieces like this for between $2,000 and $15,000. We'll look back and say, "I can't believe this painting was only $5,000 10 years ago."

Goldsmith: So you're buying some of these scene paintings. Anything else outside of coins that you think is interesting right now or that you're putting your money into?

Simmons: I like western memorabilia... things like the Wild West beer posters and old advertisements. But that's moved up a lot. I paid $1,000 for a poster in 2003. One just like it just sold for $35,000 at auction last year.

I think old Navajo weavings are basically free. I own a few of them. These can be three- to eight-foot weavings. And it took some Navajo women a year or two to make it... more than 100 years ago.

They're so tightly woven, you can pour water on them and they'll hold the water. They're just amazing.

Or you can buy Native American pottery for $15,000 to $30,000 that was made over a few days. The Navajo pottery market has soared. But the weavings are undervalued.

The other big marketing idea the Indian weaving dealers are missing is this is art made by women. At some point, this will take hold and we could see a large influx of buyers.

Goldsmith: So just in general... I know you're big into surfing. And it seems like there's a major resurgence in surf culture. Is there anything collectable in the surf world?

Simmons: If there's a surf artist that will go down as the most desired or iconic, it will be John Severson. He's the founder of *Surfer Magazine*. There are other surf artists who do a better job with realism art. But Severson has an almost semi-abstract type of art. His watercolors and oil paintings (he doesn't do many oil paintings) are absolutely, unbelievably underpriced. And John is about 80.

All the early *Surfer Magazines* are also very collectible, but especially the first five years.

And the surf culture, like you say, is one of the most passionate areas of collecting.

Goldsmith: Thanks very much, Van.

Simmons: My pleasure.

Van Simmons' Top Ideas

- Van's personal gold strategy is: 25% gold bullion, 25% gold stocks, and 50% rare coins.

- A good "starter" collectible coin is the $20 **Saint-Gaudens Grade MS-65**. People buy and sell these in quantity every day.

- Antique firearms, rock and roll posters, sports cards, fine art, and western memorabilia are all trending collectible items worth researching.

LETTERS FROM

Matt Badiali

Matt Badiali is the editor of *The Stansberry Resource Report*, a monthly advisory focused on investments in energy, metals, and other natural resources. Over the years, Matt has recorded an incredible list of triple-digit winners, like Northern Dynasty Minerals (322%), Silver Wheaton (345%), and Jinshan Gold Mines (339%).

Matt takes a "boots on the ground" approach to his research. His work has taken him to Papua New Guinea, Iraq, Hong Kong, Singapore, Haiti, Turkey, Switzerland, and many other locations around the world. He has built a huge Rolodex of the most influential people in the industry – from private financiers, leading geologists, and natural-resource analysts to billionaire hedge-fund managers.

Prior to joining Stansberry Research in 2005, Matt was a geologist for a drilling company and a consultant to an environmental company. He has appeared on Fox Business, Stansberry Radio, and other business news programs. He is also a regular contributor to *Growth Stock Wire*.

In the following essays, Matt lays out the toolkit for resource investors... identifies the least and most risky areas of the sector... and demonstrates how a single investment in this industry can pay you over and over again. He even names five of the best resource companies to consider in 2016 to hedge against inflation.

The Best Time to Invest in Natural Resources

"You're either a contrarian or a victim."

If you're already a resource investor, you've likely heard this phrase.

Coined by my friend Rick Rule – one of the greatest resource investors in the world – it captures everything you need to know about resource trends.

To make huge gains, you have to buy assets when nobody wants them – like uranium stocks in the late 1990s. This is when assets get cheap. Going against the crowd in these situations will give you a sick feeling in your gut. But that's a sign that you're probably doing the right thing.

When the crowd wakes up to the boom times that follow the bust, they'll bid up your shares to incredible heights. That's when you – the contrarian – sell out to the unfortunate victim.

That's how you make big money in resources. It has been the case for hundreds of years... and it will be the case for hundreds more.

More than any other sector, natural resources can produce gains of 1,000%, 5,000%, or even 10,000%. But you have to know what you're doing. And you have to have the right tools for the job...

Let's say you've found a specific sector – like gold or oil – that allows you to take advantage of contrarian bargains.

The greatest thing about natural-resource investing in 2016 is that much of the risk is already gone from the sector. Natural resources will always be more for speculators than long-term investors. But sometimes – like today, when most investors have already abandoned the sector – it is inherently less risky.

Look at mining, for example. The following chart is the Gold Bugs Index, which tracks the share-price movement of all the largest gold miners.

As you can see, the downtrend in gold stocks that started in 2012 has taken shares of these companies back to their lowest level in more than a decade...

Gold Bugs Index

www.stansberryresearch.com

And it isn't just the big mining companies... We use the next chart to track micro-cap or "junior" gold miners. As you can see, these stocks have been beaten-down to their lowest level in more than 15 years...

Canadian Venture Exchange Composite Index

www.stansberryresearch.com

And it isn't just miners. The oil industry is approaching a bottom, too. You can see what I mean in this chart of the Dow Jones Oil and Gas Titans Index...

Dow Jones Oil and Gas Titans Index

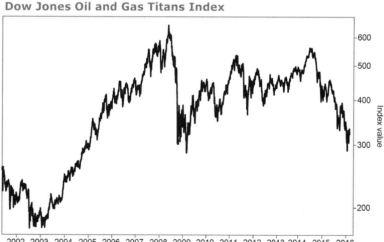

www.stansberryresearch.com

The entire commodity space is at its lowest values in decades.

The next chart is the Reuters/Jefferies Commodity (CRB) index. As you can see, this is the lowest point in 20 years...

Thompson Reuters/Jeffries Commodity Index

www.stansberryresearch.com

In short, there hasn't been this great an opportunity in natural resources in decades. The coming rally will make the bull market from 2002 to 2008 look tame by comparison. We're preparing for the kind of profits that can set us up for life.

Just a couple strategic investments could tack a zero on to your net worth. That's the kind of potential that natural-resource investing offers. And the set up today is huge...

Now you need to "get long." And the decision you have to make is **what tools to use for the job**.

There are several ways to make a bullish bet on commodities. Each has its pros and cons... its particular risks and rewards. One investment might be a great idea for some folks, but terrible for others.

I'll show you how to choose...

An Essential Toolkit for Resource Investors

When it comes to resources, we can put our trading "tools" in nine broad categories.

I'll give you a "thumbnail" overview of each category and assign it a low-risk, moderate-risk, or high-risk rating. Only experienced traders who can handle volatility should consider putting money in any of the high-risk categories.

These ratings are specific to the resource market... I'm not considering how risky any of these categories are relative to bonds, real estate, or blue-chip stocks, for example.

One more note before we begin: *There are no "safe" natural resource investments.* Whatever the rating... volatility analysis back to the 1970s shows you can see your investment fall 36%, and it's completely normal. So this sector is not for the faint of heart.

Let's get started on the "low risk" end...

Low-Risk Resource Investments

THE PHYSICAL

"If you're bullish on a given commodity and you have the means, just buy the stuff!" That's the advice you'll hear from investors who don't want to trade in and out of stocks.

The problem is... most commodities don't lend themselves to low-cost, efficient storage. Sure, you can buy 10 ounces of gold bullion and store it in a vault. But most folks don't have the means to store corn, crude oil, natural gas, uranium, or cotton.

Generally, buying the physical commodity itself only works with precious metals like gold, silver, and platinum. They have tremendous "value density." Just a handful of one-ounce coins can add up to $10,000.

So owning a stash of gold, silver, and platinum coins is a great idea, in my opinion. It's real, tangible wealth to keep on hand in case of a dollar crisis... or if you need to discreetly transfer a large amount of wealth.

THE 'BIGGIES'

In any given commodity sector, a handful of giant producers usually dominate the industry. These heavyweights have the money to hire most of the best people. They manage the biggest projects. They buy the most equipment, and their capital spending "sets the tone" for the rest of the industry.

For example, a handful of large producers mine most of the world's gold. These include Barrick, Goldcorp, Newmont, AngloGold Ashanti, and Newcrest. In the oil sector, you have ExxonMobil, Royal Dutch Shell, and Chevron (in addition to large, state-owned companies that aren't publicly traded).

The "biggies" typically have been around a long time and are fairly stable businesses. They have a mix of assets around the world. Their market caps are anywhere from $10 billion to $300 billion (depending on the industry). Many pay dividends.

This means they are less volatile than smaller companies... and are appropriate for conservative investors.

They are not without risk, however. A big fall in the price of the commodity they produce can send their shares lower. Likewise, shares might stall if increases in their costs of production outpace increases in the price of the commodity they produce.

Moderate-Risk Resource Investments

EXCHANGE-TRADED FUNDS, PART 1

When it comes to resource investing, exchange-traded funds (ETFs) come in two different "flavors"...

The first type we'll address owns a diversified basket of exploration and production firms. For example, the iShares U.S. Energy Sector Fund (IYE) owns a broad swath of oil producers, explorers, and various other energy firms. As I write, the fund owns more than 50 different energy stocks.

When it comes to gold, a popular fund is the Market Vectors Gold Miners Fund (GDX). It owns 30 different gold stocks, some large, some small.

When you own a diversified basket of stocks, you give up much of your upside. You'll also end up owning lots of "so-so" companies. But these ETFs can give you exposure to a sector without subjecting you to the risk of owning just one or two companies. These are appropriate for risk-averse investors.

ROYALTY FIRMS

This is one of my favorite categories. Royalty companies are a unique and efficient way to invest in a given resource trend.

Most royalty companies are in the gold and silver sector. But they mine no metals of their own. Instead, they finance a lot of early-stage exploration or production projects. When a mine they finance starts producing, the royalty company gets a cut of the cash flow.

Royalty companies are high-profit-margin, diversified, and leveraged ways to speculate on higher commodity prices. The large royalty firm Royal Gold, for example, climbed 23-fold from mid-2001 to 2011. The large silver royalty firm, Silver Wheaton, climbed 14-fold from its credit-crisis low in 2008 to its 2011 high.

If you buy quality royalty firms when their underlying commodities are out of favor, you can set yourself up for huge gains. But always keep in mind that their share prices can fall if their underlying commodity enters a bear market.

As I said, this is one of my favorite ways to invest in specific resources.

PICKS AND SHOVELS

Another one of my favorite ways to invest in a resource boom is with "picks and shovels." These companies provide vital equipment and services needed to explore for and extract resources.

The classic "picks and shovels" success story is set in the 1850s. Back then, a German immigrant moved from New York to San Francisco to participate in the California Gold Rush. Rather than the "all or nothing" route of looking for a big gold strike, this guy sold basic goods to the miners. He eventually started producing a new type of durable pants. They became a huge hit... and he got rich.

His name was Levi Strauss. Levi didn't risk it all on trying to find the big strike... he just sold the stuff everyone else needed to try to find the next big strike themselves.

The idea of owning "picks and shovels" has become an investment cliché for good reason. It can be an incredibly profitable, diversified way to benefit from rising commodity prices.

When it comes to modern-day picks and shovels, we have a wide variety of ideas to consider...

You have companies like Schlumberger and Halliburton. These two companies are giant "oil service" providers. They sell equipment and services to large oil companies... You have Joy Global, which sells mining equipment...

You have Core Laboratories, which performs advanced seismic research so oil companies know where to drill... You have companies like Trican Well Services and Calfrac that perform the new type of "hydraulic fracturing" services that have revolutionized North American energy production...

You have Kennametal, which sells extremely durable cutting teeth and blades to explorers... You have Bristow Group, which sells helicopter services to the offshore oil and gas industry.

The variety of picks-and-shovels choices is extraordinary. And one well-timed buy when these companies are out of favor can make for hundreds-of-percent gains. But always keep in mind that these companies boom when times are good and bust when times are not so good.

THE MID-TIER PRODUCERS

You can consider "mid-tier" producers as "biggies in training." Mid-tier producers are still relatively large companies, with market caps ranging from $1 billion to $50 billion (again, depending on the industry). But mid-tier producers typically have a narrower asset base. For example, a gold mining "biggie" might operate 10 large mines around the world, while a mid-tier producer might operate just two or three large mines.

Because mid-tier producers have less asset diversification, they're riskier than larger, more diversified companies. If a mid-tier producer has a major problem with one of its mines or oilfields, it will cause a huge swing in its profitability and a huge swing in its share price.

Still, these companies can be great investments if they have smart managers. There's more potential for growth with mid-tiers than there is with "biggies."

High-Risk Resource Investments

EXCHANGE-TRADED FUNDS, PART 2

The second "flavor" of resource ETFs is "pure play" funds. These funds trade directly in their given resource, instead of through shares (like gold fund GDX). They buy the commodity outright and/or trade futures contracts. (A futures contract is a written agreement between a buyer and seller of any commodity. The agreement specifies what is going to be sold, for how much, and when it will be delivered.)

There are funds that rise and fall in lockstep with gold and silver prices, for example. There are funds that attempt to rise and fall with oil, natural gas, and copper prices.

I'm generally not a fan of these funds. Most of them "bleed" value because they have to trade in the futures market... and they charge substantial fees.

Also, when it comes to owning "real money" assets like gold and silver, why own "digital" when you can own the real stuff?

NONPRODUCERS WITH GOOD ASSETS

"Nonproducers with good assets" is an odd class of resource stock. These are companies that own one or two large assets that could be turned into mines or oilfields... but have not been put into production for some reason or another.

Seabridge Gold is one of the highest-profile companies in this class. It owns the "KSM" project in British Columbia, Canada. KSM is one of the world's largest undeveloped gold and copper deposits. It's an absolute monster, with nearly 40 million ounces of gold and 10 billion pounds of copper in proven and probable reserves.

The problem with KSM is that it's in an inaccessible area of Canada. Huge investments in roads and electrical infrastructure are required to mine KSM. We're talking billions of dollars. Still, if gold prices were to soar, it would be worth it.

You can make good money in these types of plays if you buy them when their underlying commodity is in the pits... and on the cusp of a big rally. From 2005 to 2008, for example, Seabridge Gold rallied more than 1,000%.

But investors have to be careful buying these companies. Often, big deposits have big factors working against them... like environmental concerns, political concerns, or, in Seabridge's case, a remote location. They're among the riskiest plays in the resource market.

JUNIOR EXPLORERS

Junior explorers are the "bloodhounds" of the resource industry. Their market caps are typically in the $5 million-$100 million range, miniscule next to a "biggie." (ExxonMobil is 1,000 times larger than a $38 million "junior.")

The business model here is to find a prospective area that could be rich in metals or oil, raise money from investors, hire geologists and some drilling equipment, and look for a big strike. If it finds that big strike, the junior will sell it to a larger company.

Early investors can make 1,000%... 5,000%... even 10,000% here. But this is the "Wild West" of the resource stock world. Junior explorers are the riskiest area of the market. They are inappropriate for 99.9% of investors. They have little in the way of tangible assets. They are essentially a group of corporate managers and geologists with a dream and a story.

The vast majority burn up their cash and find nothing.

In any given industry, however, there are some folks who are habitually successful when it comes to finding big resource deposits. If you stick to investing with proven, honest managers, you can make great money in "juniors." Just keep in mind that out of a random selection of 1,000 junior explorers, fewer than 10 are worth considering as a speculation.

Again, most investors should steer clear of this market, which has less trading liquidity and lots of worthless companies masquerading as "investments."

In Summary...

When it comes to "playing" a resource trend, you have lots of tools. You have to decide for yourself how much risk and volatility you can tolerate.

In my newsletter, *Stansberry Resource Report*, we invest in a mix of "biggies," mid-tier producers, royalty firms, the physical, selected funds, and picks and shovels.

I recommend avoiding most "pure play" funds. I only recommend "juniors" to folks who are comfortable with handling risk and volatility.

You might note that I've left futures and options markets off this list. I know many folks who are successful in this area of the market, but it's totally inappropriate for most individual investors. Please only swim in these waters if you're an advanced trader.

Gold Royalties: The Secret to Huge Returns in Precious Metals

In every industry, there's usually a low-risk way to get paid over and over again for a single idea, property, or patent.

In the drug business, the big money is in patents. After all the work is done developing a new drug, for example, a scientist can partner up with a larger company to handle the expenses and risks of testing, marketing, and distribution. Then the patent holder gets paid for every prescription that gets filled.

The guy who developed the popular pain medication Lyrica, for instance, shares in more than $2 million per month... because he owns the patents. The women who owned the patents on the antifungal medicine Nystatin shared more than $50,000 per month for 20 years.

In the publishing business, the big money is in book royalties. Once you do all the work writing a book, you just sit back and collect your share of the profits. It's how President Barack Obama has more than doubled his government salary. Similarly, former President Bill Clinton makes more than $84,000 per month from sales of his bestseller, *My Life*.

You don't have to develop a new drug or write a book. There's an incredible way you can use this secret as an investor.

In short, you can own companies that avoid many of the normal risks of doing business... and get paid over and over again, simply for owning an incredibly valuable asset.

As resource investors, we want to own companies that collect royalties on the world's most vital commodities.

Let's get started...

What Are 'Royalty Companies'?

Owning royalty companies is one of the easiest and safest ways to turn a small investment into incredible wealth.

Royalty companies generate cash by selling the production of natural resources – such as oil, natural gas, coal, and precious metals.

Through these companies, you avoid many of the normal risks of finding and extracting natural resources... and simply own the companies that collect incredible streams of income.

Most royalty companies are in the gold and silver sector. But they mine no metals of their own. Instead, they finance a lot of early-stage exploration or production projects. When a mine they finance starts producing, the royalty company gets a cut of the cash flow.

Royalty companies in the energy sector don't spend capital on exploration. They don't spend it on developing projects or on maintaining them. They are built solely around income from existing projects.

Think of it this way... One company finds raw land, builds a new housing development, and then draws in people to rent. It manages the development and chases down dead-beats.

This company takes big risks. It lays out huge investments and hopes that it will eventually get its money back. But we aren't buying that kind of company.

We are essentially investing after the houses are full of renters... and we just show up on rent day and get a check for our share.

In this chapter, I'll talk about the types of royalty companies we like to buy, the different ways they're structured, and which companies should always be on your "watch list."

One of the Best Hedges Against Inflation

One way to make a lot of money with the royalty model is to invest in an industry where profits and demand are practically certain to go up.

There's just one industry that falls into this category...

This business produces an asset that has retained its purchasing power for all of recorded human history.

It's a universally recognized timeless store of value. We find its natural properties intrinsically valuable, making it well-suited to use as money: It's portable, divisible, and doesn't corrode.

I'm talking, of course, about the gold industry. It's the one place where prices and demand will continue to climb.

The U.S. government has only one way out of the giant mess it has put us in... and that's to print trillions of dollars. When the government keeps the printing presses on, inflation is right around the corner. And gold is one of the best hedges against inflation.

Gold fell 60% from its 2011 high of around $2,000 an ounce to its 2015 low of less than $1,100. But from early December 2015 to early March 2016, the metal regained nearly 20% to nearly $1,300 an ounce.

And when inflation hits, the price of gold will likely skyrocket. (Some currency analysts I respect believe gold could hit $5,000 an ounce before it's all done.)

And it's not just gold...

As governments in America and Europe create vast sums of new money... a growing number of people are turning to silver to preserve their wealth, as well.

You could take advantage of this trend by buying shares of a gold- or silver-mining company or bullion.

But one of the easiest and safest ways to turn a small investment into incredible wealth is to own royalty interests in the gold and silver industries. You avoid many of the normal risks of mining... and simply own the companies that collect incredible streams of income from royalties on the world's best precious metals mines.

This is the perfect time to invest in these companies, thanks to the recent downturn in the gold price. As you can see in the chart below, gold's long-term bull market broke in 2011.

Gold

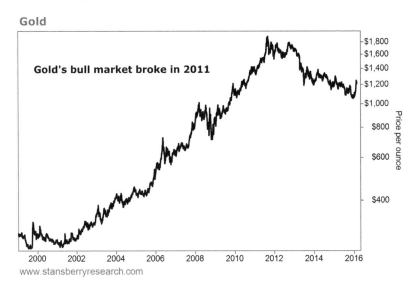

www.stansberryresearch.com

The price of gold fell rapidly from late 2012 to late 2015... and has since reversed.

As you can imagine, the recent rise in the gold price sparked big moves in gold producers. The following is a two-year chart of the Gold Bugs Index we discussed earlier. As you can see, the index climbed nearly 70% from its low in January 2016 to early March. That's great news. And mining royalty companies are leading the charge upward.

Gold Bugs Index

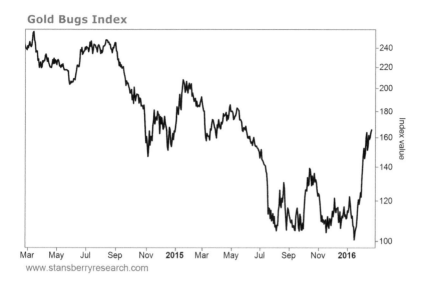

www.stansberryresearch.com

Why You Should Invest in Mining Royalties

Mining royalty companies first took shape in the late 1980s when some mining executives and industry financiers decided to find a better way to get rich in the gold-mining sector...

You see, building a large gold mine is an expensive and risky proposition.

To start, you have to pay geologists to scour the Earth in search of prospective ore bodies. You have to rent or buy pricy drilling equipment. You have to rent or buy chunks of land... often in countries you wouldn't take the family to. And you pay those governments for the proper permits and licenses.

What do you get for all this searching? Fewer than one in 3,000 "discoveries" result in an economic deposit.

Even then... if you actually find a big deposit... it can cost more than $1 billion (and sometimes much more) to build a mine. You have to raise money to pay for huge ore-processing facilities, huge dump trucks, huge excavators, huge everything. You need to hire an army of skilled workers to build and operate all that equipment. In addition, construction and permitting takes a lot of time. It can take years to build a mine, and that means years before you have anything to sell.

So around 25 years ago... a few industry insiders decided they'd had enough... They pooled their money. Then, teaming with the best resource geologists in the industry, they planned to evaluate as many ongoing exploration projects as they could find. And when they came across a top-shelf deposit likely to result in a profitable mine... they'd buy a stake in it.

You see, most mining companies are little more than a management team and a piece of land (which may or may not have minerals). They explore and assess their property... But they don't produce anything, so they don't have any earnings. And because, as I explained, mining is incredibly expensive... these companies are constantly raising money.

One way they raise money is going to the capital markets and selling shares... which they do frequently. Another way is selling a "royalty" – the rights to a portion of the mineral resource for the life of a mine.

That's how these companies buy up royalty stakes in as many of the world's best mining assets as they can.

In exchange for giving the mining company a lump-sum payment up front, the royalty company gets a paycheck for the life of the mine. A royalty company may make hundreds of small investments to spread out its risk and balance future payments.

It's a winning proposition for everyone. For cash-starved mining companies... the upfront investment from these companies provides critical capital to keep their efforts alive. Also, selling a royalty does not require a miner to issue shares. Limiting the share count means a larger piece of future earnings goes to existing shareholders.

For the royalty companies, the model eliminates many of the risks of traditional mining... They don't have to waste time and money exploring barren territory. Instead, they can hand-select the most promising prospects... and spread their risk across numerous projects. Once the mine is developed and the mining company begins repaying the investment... the income allows the royalty companies to add more and more coveted prospects to their portfolios...

The results for investors have been spectacular... Royalty companies have been among the great success stories of the stock market's recent history.

Consider Royal Gold... A penny stock with a market cap less than $50 million, Royal Gold entered the markets quietly in 1992. Research giants like Merrill Lynch and Goldman Sachs didn't know the company existed. Most mutual funds steered clear of it, too.

But after securing a portfolio of rich royalty deals... Royal Gold shares ascended from a penny stock to $100 a share. The company has generated returns of more than 100,000% since 1992. That's not a typo.

Of course, no one can predict those kinds of gains. But in my own career, I've used royalty companies to help subscribers generate big returns... In one case, we booked a 345% gain in about 18 months.

One last thing to know... The royalty business is, at its core, an intellectual business. The company's management must have the geologist's ability to tell a good mine from a bad one. It has to have the financier's ability to structure deals that offer the most benefit to both sides of the royalty... And it has to know when the time is right to raise additional capital it can deploy to benefit shareholders.

That means we want to know as much about the management and directors of our royalty companies as possible. And that's why we require a proven track record of success with our royalty investments. Investing with the right people is directly responsible for our success. However, once we find the right royalty managers, we get to invest in projects screened by the best in the industry.

Three of the best mining royalty companies in the business to consider today are Royal Gold (Nasdaq: RGLD), Franco-

Nevada (NYSE: FNV), and Osisko Gold Royalties (TSX: OR).

Silver Wheaton (NYSE: SLW) is a "streaming" company. That's like a modified royalty that requires Silver Wheaton to buy its silver and gold at steeply discounted prices. The company is also a good buy.

Finally, **Altius Minerals (TSX: ALS) is a great mining royalty company**. **It owns royalties on coal, iron ore, gold, and other minerals**. Altius is less exposed to gold than to other metals, but is still a good investment at today's prices.

All five of these companies began 2016 heading higher.

Matt Badiali's Top Ideas

- If you're bullish on a given commodity and you have the means, buy physical metals. Owning a stash of gold, silver, and platinum coins is the least-risky way to invest in natural resources. It's real, tangible wealth to keep on hand in case of a dollar crisis or if you need to discreetly transfer a large amount of wealth.

- Buying junior mining stocks is the riskiest way to invest in the gold sector. They are inappropriate for 99.9% of investors. They have little in the way of tangible assets. They are essentially a group of corporate managers and geologists with a dream and a story. That said, they have been known to soar as high as 10,000%. If you're an experienced trader who can handle volatility... it might be worth putting a small amount of money into this beaten-down sector.

- Owning royalty companies is one of the easiest and safest ways to turn a small investment into incredible wealth. Four of the best mining royalty companies in the business to consider today are Royal Gold (Nasdaq: RGLD), Franco-Nevada (NYSE: FNV), Osisko Gold Royalties (TSX: OR), and Altius Minerals (TSX: ALS).

Dan Ferris

Dan Ferris is the editor of *Extreme Value*, a monthly investment advisory that focuses on finding some of the safest, cheapest, and most profitable stocks in the market: great businesses trading at steep discounts...

Dan was among the few newsletter analysts to accurately describe the breadth and depth of the coming financial crisis in April 2008. And he told investors to get out of small-cap mining stocks in May 2011, just before they went into a brutal, multiyear bear market.

His impressive track record, candid voice, and deep research have earned him a loyal following – including more than 20 major financial firms and well-known fund managers.

Dan has appeared on *Money with Melissa Francis* and *The Willis Report* on Fox Business News, as well as *The Street* with Paul Bagnell on Business News Network. He has also been featured several times in *Barron's*, the *Value Investing Letter*, and financial radio programs around the country.

In the following essays, Dan discusses the unconventional wealth-building principles that will help you find incredible investments when the market and economy are in crisis. He shares the most important lesson you can learn to consistently make money from your investments... the five financial clues that will lower your risk and raise your returns in stocks... and his favorite example of how to identify the best values in the market.

How to Make a Fortune Outside the Wall Street System

The Wall Street system is broken.

That became obvious during the 2008 financial crisis. Not long after midnight on September 15, 2008, financial services firm Lehman Brothers declared bankruptcy – ending the 158-year existence of one of the most respected firms on Wall Street.

The next day, the U.S. government took over insurance and financial-services company AIG. That same week, Goldman Sachs and Morgan Stanley applied to the Federal Reserve to become commercial banks. They were approved within 24 hours. Since when does the government approve anything in 24 hours? Both banks needed bailout money. Neither deserved a penny.

Then Fannie Mae and Freddie Mac collapsed. A few weeks later, Washington Mutual – America's biggest savings and loan association – collapsed. While all this was happening, $7 trillion was wiped out of the stock market.

Wall Street is NOT about preserving and growing clients' hard-earned wealth. In 2008, everybody found out Wall Street is little more than a gigantic army of financial "helpers" with no idea of the difference between a great investment and a terrible one – running around, trying to get you to pour your money into the latest hot investment fad.

The banks were all pushing real estate and subprime mortgages before the crisis... You know how that turned out.

Then, even after they almost caused the global financial system to implode, the banks got bailed out and paid themselves fat bonuses. Hardly anybody from Wall Street has gone to jail for what they did during the crisis. They're still there, getting rich by charging you fees... even if you lose money.

If that doesn't sound broken to you, I don't know what would!

So... how do you beat this broken system? How do you get around the army of helpers and forge your own path to prosperity in the financial markets?

Simple. Learn how the system causes you to lose money... then do the opposite.

Look for unconventional ways of making money... that go against almost everything you'll hear from the talking heads on CNN, CNBC, or any other news channel.

The "opposite of Wall Street" types of investments I follow in my *Extreme Value* newsletter have two things in common...

First, they're extremely limited. Just a few thousand public companies are good enough for us to even consider recommending them to our readers. Second, they may not be "sexy" investments, but nearly all of them are actively making a profit at the time of our recommendation.

If you want to make a fortune in the stock market, you can't rely on your broker... your mutual-fund manager... or anyone else on Wall Street. They shove you into all the wrong investments just to benefit themselves.

The more you trade, the more commission they make... even if their clients are losing money on every trade. Paying lots of commissions means you have to make more and more on every trade just to break even. That's not the way for an investor to make money. It's far better to make a few, well-chosen, long-term investments and pay very little in commission.

In this chapter, I'll show you the most important lessons to learn about consistently making money from your investments. Let these lessons guide you, and I'm confident you'll make a fortune in the markets...

Lesson No. 1: How to Make the Stock Market Serve You

It's a popular idea on Wall Street that timing the stock market is a good way to get rich quick. Most investors have fallen for the hype...

First, most folks wind up believing the market gives "signals." It basically tells them what to buy, when to buy it, and when to sell it. They want to "follow the trend." Wall Street loves to find reasons for you to buy and sell as often as possible because it gets paid more as you trade more often.

Instead, you should focus on ways to steadily grow your wealth over the long term. You must have patience to make real money in stocks. It's that simple. The most successful investors agree...

Jesse Livermore – one of the biggest short-term traders on Wall Street in the early 20th century – said he made most of his money by "sitting" on his investments, not by buying and selling. Warren Buffett – the greatest investor of our age – once said, "Inactivity strikes us as intelligent behavior."

Second, most investors obsess about stock prices. The talking heads on CNBC encourage this behavior... They report every tiny up and down tick of the stock market, and try to assign some meaning to each one. But with long-term investing, up and down ticks in a stock's price have no real meaning. They're mostly random movements.

The best way to make the market serve you is to stop obsessing about stock prices. To teach you the proper way to approach stock market investing, we must tell the tale of Mr. Market.

Value-investment guru Benjamin Graham told the story of Mr. Market decades ago in his classic book, *The Intelligent Investor*. Graham was

Warren Buffett's mentor. He's the father of modern stock analysis.

The story goes like this...

> To succeed in the stock market, you should act like you own part of a business and your partner, named Mr. Market, also owns part of it.
>
> Mr. Market is very accommodating. He comes into work every single day and offers to buy your piece of the business at one price... and sell you his at another price. After a little while in business, you discover Mr. Market is a manic depressive. When he's manic and happy, he offers to buy your stake in the business for any price you'll name. No price is too high. When your partner is feeling sad and depressed, he seems desperate to get rid of his stake. He'll accept any price, no matter how low.
>
> When he's happy, you're wise to sell him all or part of your interest in the business. You know you can buy it back at a cheaper price when he's sad and depressed.
>
> Most of the time, Mr. Market's mood is somewhere in between the two extremes. You soon realize it's best to ignore Mr. Market, form your own ideas about what the business is worth, and not worry what he thinks.

Buying stocks is the same way. If you own shares of a business that becomes insanely expensive in the stock market, selling is often the right move. And when the market offers shares of a good business at a cheap price, buying them is the right move.

But most of the time, you should ignore the stock market... Forget the stock market even exists, and focus on the business results of each of the companies whose shares you own.

Random daily up and down stock-price movements are mostly worthless to the long-term investor. All they tell you is the price other people are buying and selling the stock for at any given moment. That has little to do with the intrinsic value of the business.

Most investors just can't ignore the market. So they behave like Mr. Market. They get happy and excited... and they pay anything to buy stocks. Eventually, stock prices stop going up. They turn around and go down. Then investors get scared and sell stocks.

These are both huge mistakes. You'll never steadily grow your wealth in the stock market by reacting to what the market is doing. You have to learn to act rationally instead of reacting emotionally...

Lesson No. 2: Learn to Act Rationally Instead of Reacting Emotionally

The first thing acting rationally means is learning to rejoice and get greedy when stock prices fall. That's when smart investors take advantage of Mr. Market and pick up bargains. Think about it. When something you want goes on sale, you tend to buy more of it. You should do the same thing in the stock market.

Learn to be cautious or even downright fearful when stock prices go up a lot and become expensive. When Mr. Market gets happy or excited, you know that he's likely to be paying too much for businesses. When Mr. Market gets depressed, it's time for us to buy stocks and sow the seeds of big future profits...

It might sound crazy, but I love it when stock prices fall. Lower stock prices create two valuable benefits for investors: They minimize risk, and they offer higher future returns.

First, risk goes up when stock prices go up. Risk goes down when stock prices go down. You always want as little risk as possible, so you should feel most relaxed and confident when stock prices are on the low side. You should start getting nervous only when stock prices have gone way up and are expensive.

Second, buying stocks when they're cheap is how you boost your gains in the market. Think about it this way... If you're buying a business that makes $1,000 a year in profit, will you make a bigger return on your investment if you pay $10,000 for the business or if you pay $20,000 for it? This is not a trick question.

You'll make 10% a year on your investment if you pay $10,000 and just 5% a year if you pay $20,000. Stocks are the same way. If you buy shares of a great business for 20 times earnings, you'll make a lower return than if you buy for 10 times earnings. You'll do even better if you buy for just five times earnings.

When stocks crashed in 1973-1974, billionaire investor Warren Buffett saw so much opportunity in the market that he said he felt like "an oversexed man in a harem." Just a few years earlier, stocks were soaring and everyone was buying them. There weren't enough cheap stocks left to buy, so Buffett shut down his investment partnership.

Great investors do the opposite of everyone else.

If you want to be a great investor – and make a fortune while other investors lose their shirts – you have to learn to buy stocks when they're cheap... even though that means going against Wall Street and buying when prices are falling.

Everyone who finds out what I do for a living has the same question for me. They all say, "What do you think the market will do?" I always say the same thing: "I don't know, and I don't care. But I hope it falls 15% or 20% so I can buy some great businesses at cheap prices."

I'm not being flippant or facetious. I mean it. I want to buy stocks. I want their prices to fall so I can get more for my money.

That's the ultimate secret to thinking the opposite of Wall Street. Ignore them. Think for yourself. The best way to do that is to focus on the value of the business you're investing in...

How to Think About Individual Stocks

Warren Buffett has said you should only buy a stock if you'd be happy to see the stock exchange shut down for 10 years while you hold onto it. Make the market serve you. Don't ask it to tell you what to do.

The key to making the market serve you is knowing how to pick the best, safest stocks that will compound your money over decades. So what is compounding, and what does it have to do with safe stocks?

For our purposes, stocks are best viewed as long-term investments, not short-term speculative vehicles. (Even the best short-term traders I know are successful primarily because they maintain a long-term outlook.)

The average investor doesn't do this. The average holding period of stocks traded on the New York Stock Exchange is less than one year. Wall Street loves to churn investors' accounts, encouraging them to buy and sell rapidly to generate big commissions.

If you want to make money, you have to ignore what Wall Street wants you to do. The longer you let an investment sit – I'm talking decades – the more your money will work to earn you even more money...

Understand this: A stock is a piece of a business. If there are 100 shares outstanding, and you own one share, you own 1% of the business. Stocks aren't lottery tickets... You don't buy them so you can cash them in at the end of the week.

It takes years for business value to grow. Few businesses grow at fast rates... and most of the ones that do turn out to be lousy investments. Take online-coupon company Groupon, for instance. From November 2011 to November 2012, Groupon sales grew 45%, but its share price still collapsed 90%.

Rapid growth is never sustainable. It's not worth anything to you as an investor if it isn't accompanied by increasing profitability. Groupon has yet to turn a profit.

So be patient, and let your investments ride. You won't be paying much in commission, and you will be growing your returns each year... Say a bank account earns 5% a year. That means you earn 5% of the amount you deposit every year. Deposit $100, and you'll have $105 by the end of the year. By the end of the second year, you'll have $110.25 ($105, plus 5% of $105), and so on.

Holding shares of a business is the same way. If you invest $100 in a business that's generating a 10% return, you'll have an investment worth $110 after one year, $121 after the second year, and so on. Over time, that really adds up.

Learn how to evaluate individual businesses so you can find the best ones where your hard-earned money will compound at the highest rates.

In the next chapter, I'll show you the five financial clues that help you find the best businesses...

Five Financial Clues to Lower Your Risk and Raise Your Returns

I've studied the financial statements of more than 20,000 public companies over the last 15 years. In that time, I've developed a brief list of five easy-to-learn financial clues that can help steer you toward investments in great businesses.

Few companies have all five clues. Even some of the best businesses in the world don't have all five. Every now and then, you'll find a company that does... but isn't right for you.

Overall, if you focus your stock market investments on companies that have all or most of them, you're well on your way to finding really great businesses you can hold for many years and compound your money at high rates of return.

Here they are...

Consistent Returns on Equity

Return on equity (ROE) is one of the most important financial clues to look at when selecting a wonderful business. It tells you how much money you're going to make (on average, over the long term) on the capital you invest in the equity of a business (for as long as that ROE holds out).

The investment equity holders make in a business is the **equity capital**. The return is the excess **cash profit** that can be taken out and distributed to them. The traditional ROE formula is net income divided by shareholder equity. I like to use some different numbers...

I use "free cash flow" for the cash profit and "tangible shareholder equity" at the beginning of the period as equity.

If a business is able to produce consistently high ROE, it can reinvest at least some of its profit and earn high returns on the new money. Think of it like a bank account... The interest you earn on your cash earns its own interest, compounding your money over time.

Well, imagine compounding your money at 10%, 20%, 30%, or even more for decades. You can't do that in any bank account. But you can by owning shares of a great business.

Automatic Data Processing (ADP) is the largest payroll processor in the U.S. It's also a great business that generates high returns on equity every year.

ADP has consistently earned 20% or more on equity since 2007. In 2015, it earned 31% on equity. And it does this without taking on debt, which is highly unusual, especially for a financial firm.

Consistent Profit Margins

Through the action of the free market, a company's profit margins usually get smaller over time. If it's a really good business, other entrepreneurs will notice the big profits it's making. And they'll try to compete with it by offering the same goods or services at a lower price... pushing profit margins lower for the entire industry.

But sometimes, you find a business where the profit margins remain at a consistent thickness year after year for many years at a time. That's the kind of business we're interested in. Consistent profit margins tell you this business has a competitive advantage over other businesses.

One of my favorite examples of this is Anheuser-Busch InBev (NYSE: BUD). It's a beer brewer that sells more than 200 brands globally, including Budweiser, Corona, and Stella Artois.

Every year since 2008, AB InBev has earned a double-digit profit of at least 11% after paying all expenses (including interest and taxes) – no matter what competitors do.

AB InBev is the No. 1 beer brewer in the world. It beats out the competition. A business needs a durable competitive advantage to stay No. 1. AB InBev's competitive advantage is a relentless focus on cutting costs and keeping them low in order to preserve its products' affordable prices.

When you find a business that earns a consistent profit margin for many years, take a deeper look. You may be looking at another AB InBev.

Gushing Free Cash Flow

A stock is a piece of a business... and businesses get their value from how much cash you can take out of them during the time you own them. So I like companies that gush free cash flow...

Free cash flow is all the cash profit left over after the company pays all its expenses and taxes, and after it reinvests enough cash to maintain and grow the business. It's a proxy for the cash you could take out of the business if you owned 100% of it. You can quickly calculate this amount by going to the cash flow statement and subtracting capital expenditures from operating cash flow.

Free cash flow =
Operating cash flow – Capital expenditures

I love businesses that earn so much free cash flow they don't know what to do with it all. Big Tech companies – like Apple, for instance – earn gobs of free cash flow. Even after they invest enough to maintain and grow their businesses, they tend to generate billions in excess cash each year. That's why they tend to have huge amounts of cash on their balance sheets. It piles up faster than they can spend it.

It can be lucrative to put your money into a business that generates lots of excess cash. Over time, if these companies keep generating excess cash, they pay more and more of it out to shareholders.

Financial Fortress Balance Sheets

Most of the time, having a great balance sheet means a company has little or no debt and lots of cash.

Suppose you had almost nine times more money in the bank as you owed on your house, car, and credit cards combined. You'd feel incredibly financially secure. That's what it's like when you find a company with a great balance sheet. It's far less likely that the company will ever get into financial trouble.

Take computer and consumer-electronics giant Apple, for instance. Recently, Apple had $216 billion in cash and securities on its balance sheet... and just $63 billion in debt. That's almost three-and-a-half times as much cash as debt.

It's like having $200,000 in mortgage, car, and credit-card debt combined... and $686,000 in cash in the bank. You'd never lose a wink of sleep worrying about money. Neither should Apple shareholders.

AB InBev is another example. I recommended the stock in 2010. Readers who took my advice are up about 161% as of March 2016. The company has $44 billion in debt and less than $7 billion in cash. That's a large amount of debt, but it's a small amount of debt relative to earnings. AB InBev's net income covers its interest expense four times over.

It's like you have $1,000 a month in mortgage, car, and credit-card debt... and about $4,000 a month in cash left over after paying all living expenses and taxes. So again, you wouldn't lose a wink of sleep.

Most of the companies we recommended in my newsletter *Extreme Value* during the crisis did very well. I recommended insurance firm W.R. Berkley (NYSE: WRB) in 2008. It went up 5% that year. It's almost impossible to find a financial stock that went up during the financial crisis. But Berkley had a great balance sheet, so I knew it would be all right.

We like stocks that allow us to sleep well at night, no matter what the stock market is doing. Finding businesses with great balance sheets is one of the best ways to do that. Invest only in companies with great balance sheets, and you'll take a lot less risk in the stock market. That usually leads to making a lot more money.

Shareholder Rewards: Dividends and Buybacks

It's great if a company earns high returns on equity, has consistent profit margins, gushes free cash flow, and has a great balance sheet. But it doesn't do investors any good if the company doesn't put some of that excess cash directly into shareholders' pockets.

There are two primary ways of rewarding shareholders: dividends and share repurchases.

Dividends come from profits (another reason to favor consistently profitable businesses). The purpose of every business is to make a profit. Few businesses are able to reinvest 100% of their profits back into the business. Many choose to pay out the excess to shareholders as dividends.

The best dividend-paying companies raise their dividends every year, sometimes for decades on end. Researchers at Ned Davis Research in Florida showed that S&P 500 companies that raised their dividends every year outperformed all other types of companies in the S&P 500 Index by dividend policy.

I recommended consumer-brands company Procter & Gamble during the financial crisis, in early 2009. The company has raised its dividend every year for 61 years. Other stocks I've recommended have also raised their dividends every year for well over a decade, like Wal-Mart (39 years), ADP (39 years), oil giant ExxonMobil (32 years), shipping-"logistics" provider Expeditors International (20 years), and health care company Johnson & Johnson (52 years).

The other way companies reward shareholders is by repurchasing their shares. When they do it right (like the companies in the previous paragraph), their share counts tend to fall over the years. That makes each remaining share more valuable. Think of it this way... Instead of cutting a pie into eight pieces, these companies cut it into four pieces. It's the same amount of pizza, but your piece is much bigger.

We like companies that return a large portion of their free cash flow to shareholders. It forces a discipline on managements to maximize the results they get with the cash they don't pay out.

If you are able to recognize businesses with high returns on equity, consistent profit margins, lots of free cash flow, a great balance sheet, and the tendency to reward shareholders, you should consider buying. You might have a huge winner on your hands.

You now know the most important principles...

1. Think "opposite" Wall Street.

2. Do plenty of research on your own to find safe stocks that will provide excellent shareholder value and compound your money over time.

How much you earn in the markets is not entirely up to you. The market goes up and down, and that affects your returns. But you have a lot of control over how much money you invest there, what kind of stocks you buy, and when you buy them.

Decide today that you're going to get greedy and take advantage of new opportunities when stock prices fall... and get cautious when stock prices are expensive. Forget about the stock market most of the time. Ignore CNBC. Forget about hot trends and sexy stock stories. Just stick to learning the difference between a great business and all the rest, starting with the financial clues we've laid out for you.

Make use of these principles, and you'll wind up taking less risk in stocks, and making more money... often at times when other investors are floundering.

The Next Great Royalty Company: A Low-Risk Shot at a '10-Bagger'

I write *Extreme Value* for one reason...

To help my readers identify the best values in the market – stocks that are trading at a ridiculous discount to what the underlying businesses are actually worth.

That's how you make hundreds-of-percent gains with limited risk.

For the last few years, I've been researching one opportunity that's undervalued and barely on the radar of Wall Street analysts.

Yet it could be five to 10 times more profitable than any of the big "World Dominator" stocks we've recommended in the past – bigger than the 98% gain my subscribers logged on Wal-Mart, the 125% gain on Berkshire Hathaway, or even the 133% gain on Intel.

This opportunity is safer than those stocks, too...

It's not a hot tech stock. It's not a tiny company with the "next big thing."

It's one of the world's best businesses – a cash-gushing enterprise that has grown its revenue more than 10-fold in a year.

Altius Minerals (TSX: ALS) could become a 10-bagger...

A Five- to 10-Bagger in the Next Several Years

Altius Minerals is a prospect-generation and royalty business.

It creates royalties for little cost by staking out original mineral prospects. It also acquires existing royalties whenever it can get them at a good price.

Altius' top geologists stake out original mineral prospects for a small amount of money. Then they find a partner who is willing to earn a percent of the prospect by taking on the financial risk of drilling enough holes to outline a full-blown mineral deposit.

Altius then earns a royalty on the eventual production from that deposit.

This business can be highly lucrative. It makes money without taking on much risk. It leaves all the risk to its partner.

Altius' first big success was staking out a uranium prospect in the Central Mineral Belt region of Newfoundland, Canada. It invested about C$650,000 to do that.

A couple years later, it sold the uranium prospect for more than $200 million. And it retained a 3% sales royalty on all the uranium and other metals that will ever be mined there. If that deposit becomes a mine, Altius will make millions in royalties.

This business model is fantastic because Altius invests only a small amount of money in each prospect and then finds a partner to spend the bulk of the capital needed to develop the prospect. Sometimes, Altius creates a new public company to do that.

As of March 2016, Altius has about half-a-dozen mineral prospects with partners and another half-a-dozen in search of partners. Any one of them could be another huge winner.

Between growing its royalty income through acquisition, creating royalties, and selling mineral prospects... Altius could become a multibillion-dollar market cap company in the next several years.

Remember, Franco-Nevada is the biggest precious metals royalty company, and it has about a $9 billion market cap. Altius operates in diversified mining, not precious metals, so it could become much larger even than Franco-Nevada.

Altius' market cap in March 2016 is about C$350 million. A C$3.5 billion market cap (**about 10 times your money from here**) isn't such a crazy prospect for Altius over the next several years.

You aren't likely to make 10 times your money on Franco-Nevada. It's too late for that. But you might do it with Altius, since it's small, brilliantly managed, and has launched into royalty growth mode at the perfect moment.

Altius endured a dramatic selloff in 2015, along with the rest of the market. I don't know how long it will stay cheap. It started to rebound in early 2016... climbing 25% in three weeks from its February 11 low.

Now is a fantastic time to buy it.

The Market Still Doesn't Get It... and That's a Good Thing for You

When we first recommended Altius Minerals in early 2009, I saw a stock trading at a discount to cash and securities, with upside potential in prospect generation.

Back then, during the darkest depths of the financial crisis, the market was distracted from stocks like Altius. The market's misunderstanding and fear was our opportunity. We took advantage.

In 2016, it has much bigger cash flows, as we've described, and it knows how to deploy them. Big profits lie ahead for investors because the market still doesn't seem to get it, creating an opportunity for you to buy a great company on the cheap.

My latest calculations assign Altius an intrinsic value of roughly C$12.78 per share... not including its non-producing royalties or other liabilities.

If you value Altius by simply comparing it to the biggest nondiversified royalty company, Franco-Nevada, it would be worth about 20 times royalties (in March 2016), or around C$19 per share. That's much more than the maximum price we recommend paying for Altius of C$14 per share.

I assumed C$38 million in annual royalty revenue. That's the low end of the $38 million-$40 million range the company expects in royalty revenue for 2016.

The following table is my net asset value estimate for Altius Minerals...

Assets	Estimated Value
Cash	C$18M
Receivables	C$4.2M
Securities, including Alderon	C$28M
All producing royalties at 15x royalties	C$547M
Carbon Development Partnership at cost, less value of CDP royalties	C$34M
Extreme Value gross asset value estimate	C$631M
Total liabilities	C$96.8M
Extreme Value NAV estimate	C$534.4M
Fully diluted share count	39.93M
Per-share NAV estimate	C$13.38
Coal royalty impairment	C$0.60
New per-share adjusted NAV estimate*	**C$12.78**

*Adjusted NAV because we don't include a valuation for Altius' exploration assets, carried on its latest balance sheet at C$32 million (around C$0.80/share). They have value, but we'd rather not pay for them until they become a paying royalty or a stake in a public company.

Source: Altius public filings and reports

Altius is a diversified royalty consolidator and a fast-growing cash gusher. It owns several high-quality, long-lived assets paying tens of millions of dollars each year – *none of which will ever require another dime of capital investment to maintain*. But its cheap share price tells me the market doesn't get that.

The market doesn't understand that co-founder and CEO Brian Dalton and his team are the best capital allocators in the prospect-generation and royalty-creation space. The market doesn't understand the mistakes other prospect generators make or that Altius simply doesn't make them.

The fact that the market doesn't get it is good for us. Oaktree Capital Management Co-Founder Howard Marks has taught me to look for a consensus view in the market. If you find one, there might be an opportunity to take a different and superior viewpoint, generating an outsized investment profit.

At nine times 2015's estimated royalties and with virtually zero credit for its other assets, the market's consensus on Altius is that it's doing OK, but it's nothing special.

Altius is one of a handful of the greatest natural resource companies to ever exist. We'll see if time makes us right and you rich.

Dan Ferris' Top Ideas

- Look for unconventional ways of making money that go against almost everything you'll hear from the talking heads on CNN, CNBC, or any other news channel.

- The best way to make the market serve you is to stop obsessing about stock prices and to learn the proper way to approach stock market investing. Read *The Intelligent Investor* by Ben Graham.

- One of Dan's favorite business models is undervalued royalty companies... His top recommendation in the space is a business that he says could become a multibillion-dollar market cap company in the next several years: Altius Minerals (TSX: ALS).

LETTERS FROM

Dr. Ron Paul

Former U.S. congressman and three-time presidential candidate Dr. Ron Paul is a leading voice for liberty, prosperity, and peace in America. During his 12 terms in congress, he fought for constitutional government, low taxes, free markets, and a return to sound monetary policies.

In 2014, he partnered with Stansberry Research to bring to light what the bureaucrats in Washington – who built careers on concealing the truth – have attempted to sweep under the rug...

Since 2002, Dr. Paul has warned that Americans would become poorer and more dependent on the government to put food on the table... that the erosion of civil liberties would continue under the false flag of "National Security"... and that this country could face a real estate meltdown and financial crisis. Each of his warnings has come true.

Like Porter and the Stansberry Research team, Dr. Paul believes we're headed toward "the next great collapse," which could be far worse than the economic crisis of 2008.

In the following chapter – originally published on his "Peace and Prosperity" blog – Dr. Paul discusses what he calls "the real war on the middle class." He also offers personal advice on what to do with your money in 2016 to prepare for a monetary collapse.

The Real War on the Middle Class

One of the great ironies of American politics is that most politicians who talk about helping the middle class support policies that, by expanding the welfare-warfare state, are harmful to middle-class Americans.

Eliminating the welfare-warfare state would benefit middle-class Americans by freeing them from exorbitant federal taxes, including the Federal Reserve's inflation tax.

Politicians who are serious about helping middle-class Americans should allow individuals to opt out of Social Security and Medicare by not having to pay payroll taxes if they agree to never accept federal retirement or health care benefits.

Individuals are capable of meeting their own unique retirement and health care needs if the government stops forcing them into one-size-fits-all plans.

Middle-class families with college-age children would benefit if government got out of the student-loan business. Government involvement in higher education is the main reason tuition is skyrocketing and so many Americans are graduating with huge student-loan debts. College graduates entering the job market would benefit if Congress stopped imposing destructive regulations and taxes on the economy.

Politicians who support an interventionist foreign policy are obviously not concerned with the harm inflicted on the middle-class populations of countries targeted for regime change. These politicians also disregard the harm U.S. foreign policy inflicts on Americans.

Middle- and working-class Americans and their families who join the military suffer when they are maimed or killed fighting in unjust and unconstitutional wars. Our interventionist foreign policy also contributes to the high tax burden imposed on middle-class Americans.

Middle-class Americans also suffer from intrusions on their liberty and privacy, such as not being able to board an airplane unless they submit to invasive and humiliating searches. Even children and the physically disabled are not safe from the Transportation Security Administration. These assaults are justified by the threat of terrorism, a direct result of our interventionist foreign policy that fosters hatred and resentment of Americans.

Some "military Keynesians" claim that middle-class workers benefit from jobs in the military-industrial complex. Military Keynesians seem to think that the resources spent on militarism would disappear if the Pentagon's budget were cut.

The truth is, if we reduced spending on militarism, those currently employed by the military-industrial complex would be able to find new jobs producing goods desired by consumers. Even those currently employed as lobbyists for the military-industrial complex may be able to find useful work.

Few things would benefit the middle class more than ending the Federal Reserve. The Federal Reserve's inflationary policies erode middle-class families' standards of living while benefiting the financial and political elites. Middle-class Americans may gain some temporary benefits from booms created by the Federal Reserve, but they also suffer from the inevitable busts.

Other economies are moving away from using the dollar as the reserve currency, and this trend will accelerate as the Federal Reserve continues to pump more fiat currency into the economy and as resentment toward our foreign policy grows. Eventually, international investors will lose confidence in the U.S. economy... and the dollar bubble will burst.

These events will cause a major economic downturn that may even be worse than the Great Depression. The main victims of this crisis will be average Americans. The only way to avoid this calamity is for the American people to force Congress to free them from the burdens of the warfare state, the welfare state, taxation, and fiat currency.

'Two Percent Inflation' and the Fed's Mandate

Over the last 100 years, the Fed has had many mandates and policy changes in its pursuit of becoming the chief central economic planner for the United States. Not only has it pursued this utopian dream of planning the U.S. economy and financing every boondoggle conceivable in the welfare/warfare state, it has become the manipulator of the currency.

As former Fed Chairman Ben Bernanke explained to me, the once profoundly successful world currency – gold – was no longer money. This meant that he believed, and the world has accepted, the fiat dollar as the most important currency of the world, and the U.S. has the privilege and responsibility for managing it.

He might even believe, along with his Fed colleagues, both past and present, that the fiat dollar will replace gold for millennia to come. I remain unconvinced.

At its inception, the Fed got its marching orders: to become the ultimate lender of last resort to banks and business interests. And to do that, it needed an "elastic" currency.

The supporters of the new central bank in 1913 were well aware that commodity money did not "stretch" enough to satisfy the politician's appetite for welfare and war spending. A printing press and computer, along with the removal of the gold standard, would eventually provide the tools for a worldwide fiat currency.

We've been there since 1971 and the results are not good.

Many modifications of policy mandates occurred between 1913 and

1971. The Fed continues in a desperate effort to prevent the total unwinding and collapse of a monetary system built on sand. A storm is brewing. When it hits, it will reveal the fragility of the entire world's financial system.

The Fed and its friends in the financial industry are frantically hoping their next mandate or strategy for managing the system will continue to bail them out of each new crisis.

The seeds were sown with the passage of the Federal Reserve Act in December 1913. The lender of last resort would target special beneficiaries with its ability to create unlimited credit. It was granted power to channel credit in a special way...

Average citizens, struggling with a mortgage or a small business about to go under, were not the Fed's concern. Commercial, agricultural, and industrial paper was to be bought when the Fed's friends were in trouble and the economy needed to be propped up. At its inception, the Fed was not given permission to buy speculative financial debt or U.S. Treasury debt.

It didn't take long for Congress to amend the Federal Reserve Act to allow the purchase of U.S. debt to finance World War I and subsequently all the wars to follow. These changes eventually led to trillions of dollars being used in the current crisis to bail out banks and mortgage companies that were in over their heads with derivative speculations and worthless mortgage-backed securities.

It took a while to go from a gold standard in 1913 to the unbelievable paper bailouts that occurred during the crash of 2008 and 2009.

In 1979, Congress proposed a dual mandate to solve the problem of high inflation and high unemployment, which defied the conventional wisdom of the Phillips curve that supported the idea that inflation could be a trade-off for decreasing unemployment.

The stagflation of the 1970s was an eye-opener for all the establishment and government economists. None of them had anticipated the serious financial and banking problems in the 1970s that concluded with high interest rates.

That's when Congress instructed the Fed to follow a "dual mandate" to achieve, through monetary manipulation, a policy of "stable prices" and "maximum employment."

The goal was to have Congress wave a wand and – presto! – the problem would be solved... without the Fed giving up power to create money out of thin air that allows it to guarantee bailouts for its Wall Street friends and the financial markets.

The dual mandate was really a triple mandate. The Fed was also instructed to maintain "moderate long-term interest rates." "Moderate" was not defined. I now have personally witnessed nominal interest rates as high as 21% and rates below 1%.

The dual, or the triple, mandate has only compounded the problems we face today. Temporary relief was achieved in the 1980s and confidence in the dollar was restored after Volcker raised interest rates up to 21%. But structural problems remained.

Nevertheless, the stock market crashed in 1987 and the Fed needed more help. President Reagan's Executive Order 12631 created the President's Working Group on Financial Markets, also known as the Plunge Protection Team.

This executive order gave more power to the Federal Reserve, Treasury, Commodity Futures Trading Commission, and the Securities and Exchange Commission to come to the rescue of Wall Street if market declines got out of hand.

Though their friends on Wall Street were bailed out in the 2000 and 2008 panics, this new power obviously did not create a sound economy. Secrecy was of the utmost importance to prevent the public from seeing just how this "mandate" operated and exactly who was benefiting.

Since 2008, real economic growth has not returned. From the viewpoint of the central economic planners, wages aren't going up fast enough, which is like saying the currency is not being debased rapidly enough. That's the same explanation they give for prices not rising fast enough as measured by the government-rigged Consumer Price Index ("CPI").

In essence, it seems like they believe that making the cost of living go up for average people is a solution to the economic crisis. Rather bizarre!

The obsession now is to get price inflation up to at least 2% per year. The assumption is that if the Fed can get prices to rise, the economy will rebound. This, too, is monetary policy nonsense.

If the result of a congressional mandate placed on the Fed for moderate and stable interest rates results in interest rates ranging from 0% to 21%, then believing the Fed can achieve a healthy economy by getting consumer prices to increase by 2% per year is a pie-in-the-sky dream. Money managers CAN'T do it. And if they could, it would achieve nothing except compounding the errors that have been driving monetary policy for 100 years.

A mandate for 2% price inflation is a goal not only for the central planners in the United States but also for most central bankers worldwide.

It's interesting to note that the idea of a 2% inflation rate was conceived 25 years ago in New Zealand to curtail double-digit price inflation. The claim was made that since conditions improved in New Zealand after the government lowered the country's inflation rate to 2%, there was something magical about it.

From this, the government assumed that anything lower than 2% must be a detriment and the inflation rate must be raised. Of course, the only tool central bankers have to achieve this rate is to print money and hope it flows in the direction of raising the particular prices that the Fed wants to raise.

One problem is that although newly created money by central banks does inflate prices, the central planners can't control which prices will increase or when it will happen. Instead of consumer prices rising, the price inflation may go into other areas, as determined by millions of individuals making their own choices. There could be high prices for stocks, bonds, educational costs, medical care, and food, yet the CPI would stay under 2%.

The CPI, though the Fed currently wants it to be even higher, is misreported on the low side. The Fed's real goal is to make sure there is no opposition to the money printing press it needs to run at full speed to keep the financial markets afloat. This is for the purpose of propping up particular stock prices, debt derivatives, and bonds to take care of the Fed's friends on Wall Street.

This "mandate" that the Fed follows, unlike others, is of its own creation. No questions are asked by the legislators, who are always in need of monetary inflation to paper over the debt run up by welfare/warfare spending.

There will be a day when future economic historians will laugh at the obsession with the goal of zero interest rates and 2% price inflation. It will be considered just as silly as John Law's inflationary scheme in the 18th century for perpetual wealth for France by creating the Mississippi bubble – which ended in disaster...

After a mere two years (1719-1720) of runaway inflation, Law was forced to leave France in disgrace. The current scenario will not be precisely the same as with this giant bubble, but the consequences will likely be much greater than that which occurred with the bursting of the Mississippi bubble.

The fiat dollar standard is worldwide, and nothing similar has ever existed before. The Fed and all the world central banks now endorse the monetary principles that motivated John Law in his goal of a new paradigm for French prosperity.

His thesis was simple: First, increase paper notes to increase the money supply in circulation. This, he claimed, would revitalize the finances of the French government and the French economy. His theory was no more complicated than that.

This is exactly what the Federal Reserve has been attempting to do for the past six years. It has created $4 trillion of new money and used it to buy government Treasury bills and $1.7 trillion of worthless home mortgages. Real growth and a high standard of living for a large majority of Americans have not occurred, whereas the Wall Street elite have done well. This has resulted in aggravating the persistent class warfare that has been going on for some time.

The Fed has failed at following its many mandates, whether legislatively directed or spontaneously decided upon by the Fed itself – like the 2% price inflation rate. But in addition, to compound the mischief caused by distorting the much-needed market rate of interest, the Fed is much more involved than just running the printing presses. It regulates and manages the inflation tax.

The Fed was the chief architect of the bailouts in 2008. It facilitates the accumulation of government debt, whether it's to finance wars or the welfare transfer programs directed at both rich and poor.

The Fed provides a backstop for the speculative derivatives dealings of the banks considered "too big to fail." Together with the FDIC's insurance for bank accounts, these programs generate a huge moral hazard, while the Fed obfuscates monetary and economic reality.

The Federal Reserve reports that it has more than 300 PhDs on its payroll. There are hundreds more in the district banks and more associated scholars under contract at many universities. The exact cost to get all this wonderful advice is unknown.

The Federal Reserve, on its website, assures the American public that these economists "represent an exceptional diverse range of interest in specific area of expertise." Of course, this is with the exception that gold is of no interest to them in their hundreds and thousands of papers written for the Fed.

This academic effort by subsidized, learned professors ensures that our college graduates are well-indoctrinated in the ways of inflation and economic planning. As a consequence, too, essentially all members of Congress have learned these same lessons.

Fed policy is a hodgepodge of monetary mismanagement and economic interference in the marketplace. Sadly, little effort is being made to seriously consider real monetary reform, which is what we need.

That will only come after a major currency crisis.

I have frequently made the point about the error of central banks assuming that they know exactly what interest rates best serve the economy and at what rate price inflation should be. The obsession with a 2% increase in the CPI per year and a 0% rate of interest is rather silly.

In spite of all the mandates, flip-flopping on policy, and irrational regulatory exuberance... all central bankers share an overwhelming fear on which they dwell day and night. That is the dreaded possibility of DEFLATION.

A major problem is that of defining the terms commonly used. It's hard to explain a policy dealing with deflation when Keynesians claim a falling average price level – something hard to measure – is deflation... and the Austrian free-market school describes deflation as a decrease in the money supply.

The hysterical fear of deflation is because deflation is equated with the 1930s Great Depression. All central banks now are doing everything conceivable to prevent that from happening again through massive monetary inflation. Though the money supply is rapidly rising and some prices, like oil, are falling, we are NOT experiencing deflation.

Under today's conditions, fighting the deflation phantom only prevents the needed correction and liquidation from decades of an inflationary/mal-investment bubble economy.

Even though there's a lot of monetary inflation being generated, not much is going where the planners would like it to go. Economic growth is stagnant, and lots of bubbles are being formed, like in stocks, student debt, oil drilling, and other sectors. Our economic planners don't realize it but they are having trouble with centrally controlling individual "human action."

Real economic growth is hindered by a rational and justified loss of confidence in planning business expansions. This is a consequence of the chaos caused by the Fed's encouragement of over-taxation, excessive regulations, and diverting wealth away from domestic investments toward wealth-consuming, dangerous, and unnecessary wars overseas.

Without the Fed monetizing debt, these excesses would not occur.

Lessons Yet to Be Learned

1. Increasing money and credit by the Fed is not the same as increasing wealth. It, in fact, does the opposite.

2. More government spending is not equivalent to increasing wealth.

3. Liquidation of debt and correction in wages, salaries, and consumer prices is not the monster that many fear.

4. Corrections, allowed to run their course, are beneficial and should not be prolonged by bailouts with massive monetary inflation.

5. People spending their own money is far superior to the government spending it for them.

6. Propping up stock and bond prices is not a road to economic recovery.

7. Though bailouts help the insiders and the elite 1%, they hinder economic recovery.

8. Production and savings should be the source of capital needed for economic growth.

9. Monetary expansion can never substitute for savings, but guarantees mal-investment.

10. Market rates of interest are required to provide for the economic calculation necessary for growth and reversing an economic downturn.

11. Wars provide no solution to a recession/depression. Wars only make a country poorer while war profiteers benefit.

12. Bits of paper with ink on them or computer entries are not money – gold is.

13. Higher consumer prices per se have nothing to do with a healthy economy.

14. Lower consumer prices should be expected in a healthy economy, as we experienced with computers, TVs, and cell phones.

All this effort by thousands of planners in the Federal Reserve, Congress, and the bureaucracy to achieve a stable financial system and healthy economic growth has failed.

It must be the case that it has all been misdirected. And just maybe, a free market and a limited-government philosophy are the answers for sorting it all out without the economic planners setting interest- and CPI-rate increases.

A simpler solution to achieving a healthy economy would be to concentrate on providing a "SOUND DOLLAR," as the founders of the country suggested.

A gold dollar will always outperform a paper dollar in duration and economic performance while holding government growth in check.

This is the only monetary system that protects liberty while enhancing the opportunity for peace and prosperity.

Dr. Paul's Outlook and Advice for 2016

Since the 2008 financial crisis, we've seen a lot of money printing, but we haven't seen any real economic growth.

People are constantly asking if we're "going into a recession." I'd argue this is a continuation of the past recession being papered over. It's just more evidence the government's loose monetary policy will continue. And it's going to get much, much worse.

Eventually, we need to see a correction. It's absolutely necessary because we have too much debt and mal-investment. And you can't have economic growth unless you correct the mistakes of the previous cycle, liquidating bad debt and getting rid of mal-investment.

All the officials – whether at the Fed or in the government – are resisting this downtrend. They're in a sort of stalemate. But the market is heading down. And it's going to be a prolonged decline until there's a cataclysmic end where people throw in the towel. And that will be the point when people start to reject the dollar.

Until that happens, **I suspect the Fed will engage in a fourth round of quantitative easing ("QE")**.

You'd think the Fed would wise up and realize QE didn't do any good. But it has been following policies that haven't done much good for a long time: Spending more money, running up more debt, printing more money, pegging interest rates low... Yet it continues. I suspect the Fed will never quit inflating.

But the Fed doesn't have many tools left. It's in a box... No matter what it does, it will be wrong. So I don't believe another round of QE will be helpful in any way.

The economy is in bad shape today, but it has been papered over. Stocks have been rising, real estate prices are strong, and the dollar is strong... Still, people see unemployment growth and many Americans are having a hard time making ends meet.

Politicians and central bankers are incapable of doing the correct thing, which is to get their hands off. Let the market handle this. Get rid of the bad stuff so we can see some economic growth. Even with government intervention, we'll see liquidation of debt and corrections.

But governments actually believe they're capable of managing the economy. And they will continue to do it. The only tool they have is printing a lot of money.

I'm sure central bankers are concerned about this. But they'll never concede that their entire experiment with paper money and central banking has been a total failure. So they'll resort to something. And that will be higher government spending, more debt, and more printing of money.

By the end of 2016, it will likely be evident their efforts have failed. And they'll try to prop up the economy with more QE.

While the dollar is strong today, I'd ask "compared to what?" The answer is compared to other currencies. We're doing a little bit better because we still have economic wealth and the world's reserve currency. But ultimately, the dollar can't be a haven.

If you look at the ultimate currency that protects a person – gold – versus the dollar since 2000, you'll see a clear trend. Gold will only become more desirable as the Fed continues its massive, monetary experiment.

Not too many people realize this now, but there will be a limitation on the dollar. Nothing guarantees that we will be able to issue the reserve currency of the world. And it's eventually going to fail.

But all the currencies are liable to fail together because we're so interlocked. Our debt problem is a global problem. There's no historic event that gives insight on how this problem will play out. But when people finally give up on the dollar, they're going to give up on all paper currencies. That's when we'll see a rush for the exits.

At that point, people will want to own something of real value, whether that's metals or property.

No matter what the government tells you, the purchasing power of the dollar is falling. So while the government is trying to get the inflation rate up to 2%, why is the average person short of money at the end of the month?

Wages have been stagnant to slowly rising, but everybody seems to be short paying their bills. And that's because of the deception of government. The government is silently stealing from American citizens by debasing the currency. Not to mention, it doesn't talk much about rising medical care or education costs.

People will wake up one day and realize the dollar is not a haven. I personally don't believe it is. I would much rather hold real money than the dollar, even if the dollar is stronger.

But people aren't prepared for this event. And it's going to be horrendous. That's why I try to get people to look at this carefully... to figure out the best thing they can do to protect their wealth, their family, and their security.

People will try to protect their families by using metals as money. Gold is a haven, but what happens if you have a gold coin and the government says there's an 80% tax on it? It's much easier to tax gold like that than to confiscate it.

The government is financing its huge debt by debasing the currency and printing a lot of money. But there will be a day when that won't work, so the government will turn to confiscation.

We'll see capital controls. In some ways, they've already been introduced. The government knows everything about your transactions of currencies and finances internationally. The government should do something like not tax all the money corporations hold overseas right now and let it come home.

But there are a couple things you can do today to protect yourself from the bleak times on the horizon...

It's smart for the average person to have a trade. No matter what the conditions are around the world, there are some things in life you always need. You always need a plumber. You always need a carpenter.

Even today, with our spotty job market, people with a good trade can get good-paying jobs. So people should always think along those lines of what can they do on their own.

Farming could be the ultimate trade – especially if you own the land. Plus, with farming, you can be completely self-sustaining.

Let's say my concerns for chaos don't come to fruition for five or 10 years. I hope we have that amount of time... But regardless of the time frame, you should focus on your investments.

Some investments are more complicated than others. That's one reason hard assets like gold and real estate are good – they're simple. Again, it's important for people to have a trade like plumbing or farming.

When the hard times come and we have to focus on survival, it's also important to understand how you can bring like-minded, trustworthy people together. For example, we want as many people as possible to own gold. The more people are protected by gold, the more those people will work together. And the more they can stand up to the government.

Let me tell you a personal anecdote about having hard assets in a time of crisis...

My grandfather came from Germany alone as a 14-year-old boy. He ended up owning a five-acre farm. When he died, he left that land to my grandmother. My dad helped her with her finances. And I remember one conversation they had...

My dad asked his mother why she didn't just sell the farm. It would put money in the bank to help her take care of herself... She needed retirement income.

But she said no... "I'm going to hold onto this land in case the money goes bad." I figured she must have had experience with this kind of thing from the 1920s in Germany.

And, sure enough, I learned that my grandmother had made a trip to Germany in the '20s, during hyperinflation. So she knew about inflation. And she knew you should own land during a crisis because her relatives that owned land during that period did much better than people with money in the bank – where the government can destroy its value.

Remember, the government can steal your money through runaway inflation. It doesn't need to stick a gun in the banker's ribs to get your money. The government robs you constantly by the devaluation of money.

That's the environment we live in today.

Dr. Ron Paul's Top Ideas

- Countries are moving away from using the U.S. dollar as the reserve currency. This trend will accelerate as the Federal Reserve continues to pump more fiat currency into the economy and as resentment toward our foreign policy grows.

  Eventually, international investors will lose confidence in the U.S. economy and the bubble will burst.

- Bits of paper with ink on them or computer entries are not money – gold is.

- Learn a trade.

Looking Around

By the Stansberry Research team

We're not the only ones worried about the economy...

Some of the richest and most powerful financiers in the world are preparing for a major market correction. In addition to their public appearances, where they'll often "talk their book," you can also see exactly what moves these money managers are making...

Analysts at Stansberry Research are expected to study the buying patterns of the world's most successful hedge funds and individual investors.

Why? If you want to get better at anything, it's a great idea to study the best.

Billionaires have a keen ability to think and act differently than the average investor. Some have built their careers on buying when everyone else is selling. And while you should never blindly copy billionaires' portfolios, it can be useful to watch where they put their money.

In this section, we've included a few notes on what some of the world's richest investors are saying and doing in the markets in 2016.

Keep in mind... the following are not trading recommendations.

What Are the 'Masters of the Universe' Doing With Their Cash?

Warren Buffett (Net Worth: $65.2 Billion)
CEO, Berkshire Hathaway

No list of billionaires would be complete without "the Oracle of Omaha."

Warren Buffett's holding company, Berkshire Hathaway, owns everything from car dealerships to homebuilders to Dairy Queen restaurants. It's a bellwether for the U.S. economy. As such, Berkshire had a rough 2015. It lost nearly $11 billion.

Still, Buffett is sitting on billions more in cash. And he's already deploying that capital in the beaten-down energy sector.

He poured nearly $5 billion into shares of oil giant **Phillips 66 (NYSE: PSX)**, making Buffett its largest shareholder.

Carl Icahn (Net Worth: $19 Billion)
Founder, Icahn Capital Management

In September 2015, Icahn – one of the richest men in the world – released a 15-minute video online.

It warned individual investors about the coming losses in the high-yield bond market. In the video, Icahn said the "middle-class investor has nowhere to go with their money but into the stock market, or even more concerning, high-yield bonds, which are very risky."

In a later interview, he added, "If and when there is a real problem in the economy, there is going to be a rush to the exits like in a movie theater. We are going to go off a cliff."

Investors had loaded up on junk bond exchange-traded funds (ETFs), expecting daily liquidity. Meanwhile, the asset the ETFs were buying – risky corporate debt – is less liquid... especially during times of crisis.

In 2016, the founder and chairman of Icahn Capital Management is loading up on energy investments. He owns about 12% of **Cheniere Energy (NYSE: LNG)** and has two of his people positioned on the board of directors. He also owns mining giant **Freeport-McMoRan (NYSE: FCX)**.

The resource market is brutal. But Icahn is no stranger to a fight. He has made a fortune taking control of troubled companies and fixing their finances.

David Tepper (Net Worth: $11.4 Billion)
President and Founder, Appaloosa Management

Tepper is a distressed-debt expert whose trades following the 2008 market crash can arguably be labeled the greatest trades ever made.

He made massive investments in Bank of America and Citigroup, which had been left for dead in the height of the market panic. Tepper bet that the U.S. government wouldn't let these banks fail... and he was right. His fund returned 133% that year, earning $7 billion.

In late 2010, when the government announced a second round of quantitative easing, Tepper went long again, shifting his bond-focused fund into equities. He was famously quoted as saying, "What, I'm going to say, 'No, Fed, I disagree with you, I don't want to be long equities'?"

In 2015 – with Europe, Japan, and China joining in on their own forms of easing – Tepper added, "If it's hard to fight the Fed, it's even more difficult to fight four Feds."

Tepper knew that being long stocks was the right bet. Stocks were in a "win-win" scenario. They would head higher if the economy was actually recovering. And they would head higher if the economy stumbled because the Fed would step in with further easing. In December 2013, he said his biggest fear was not being "long enough" in stocks.

All told, Appaloosa Management returned an average of 34% a year from 1993 through 2014.

According to Reuters, Tepper's "$18.6 billion hedge fund has routinely delivered returns so strong that the manager has periodically returned capital to investors because the fund was getting too large."

In the fourth quarter of 2015, Appaloosa Management made big bets on the beaten-down energy sector.

It purchased 9.4 million shares of **Kinder Morgan (NYSE: KMI)**, 4.3 million shares of natural gas and exploration company **Southwestern Energy (NYSE: SWN)**, 3.5 million shares of natural resource company **Freeport-McMoRan (NYSE: FCX)**, and 2.3 million shares of energy and communications company **Williams Partners (NYSE: WPZ)**.

It's too early to label these trades a success, but it's a growing trend.

Many of the world's greatest investors are buying high-quality energy companies whose shares have been beaten down. These companies own one-of-a-kind "trophy assets" but trade at dirt-cheap valuations in early 2016. Eventually, the downtrend will reverse course... and we'll see huge gains.

Dan Loeb (Net Worth: $2.6 Billion)
Founder, Third Point

Activist investor Dan Loeb is just as well-known for his scathing letters to management as he is for Third Point's astounding returns.

The $17.5 billion fund has delivered average returns of 16.2% a year over the past two decades. Loeb typically takes a large position in a single firm and then agitates for a board seat. From his new position of authority within the firm, he tries to cut costs and right the ship.

Loeb has taken major stakes in businesses like Yahoo, Sony, Dow Chemical, and Amgen in the past. He also made a fortune buying distressed Greek debt. But in 2016, he's loading on short sales – though he still maintains many long positions.

"A renewed focus on generating alpha on both sides of the portfolio has led us to increase single-name equity shorts by four-fold over the past year. Our total equity short exposure is nearly $4.5 billion today," Loeb wrote in a letter to clients dated February 12, 2016.

Loeb, like most investors, is worried about China's slowdown, plummeting commodity prices, a high-yield credit correction, and soaring debt.

He says the declines we've seen to date "actually fail to capture the true carnage revealed when you take a closer look at the breadth of S&P 500 companies experiencing massive losses."

Paul Singer (Net Worth: $2.2 Billion)
Founder, Elliott Management

Paul Singer is one of the most outspoken hedge-fund managers on Earth.

He is a vocal opponent of the Fed's monetary actions... a noted gold bull... and is also one of the "toughest" managers on the Street. He famously seized an Argentine naval ship, claiming the country owed him $1.6 billion.

In 2015, Singer wrote a letter to the public, which included a bold warning about the markets…

> Today, six-and-a-half years after the collapse of Lehman, there is a Bigger Short cooking. That Bigger Short is long-term claims on paper money (i.e., bonds). History shows that it is fiendishly difficult to preserve the value of money, which is backed by nothing but promises, because it is so tempting for rulers to debase their currency when they think it will help them repay their debts.
>
> The long-term preservation of the real value (i.e., the purchasing power) of fiat money and bonds is obviously of little or no importance to today's creators of money – the major central banks – who currently can't debase money fast enough for their tastes. Yet, the current prices of bonds are at all-time highs, and thus yields are at record lows.

Singer's hedge fund has been loading up on shares of lightweight-metals manufacturer **Alcoa (NYSE: AA)**. As of March 2016, Elliott Management owns more than 6% of the company. And it's supporting the board in an effort to split the company in two. In a filing with the Securities and Exchange Commission, Elliott noted that the company was "drastically undervalued."

Jeffrey Gundlach (Net Worth: $1.38 Billion)
CEO, DoubleLine Capital

Dubbed "The Bond God," DoubleLine Capital founder Jeffrey Gundlach has earned the nickname.

He correctly predicted that oil prices and junk bonds would fall. He said China's slowing economy would hurt emerging markets and commodity prices. And he has been betting on – and profiting from –

lower interest rates. As a result, his company's assets have swelled to $85 billion.

In 2016, Gundlach is worried. The debt guru warned, "This is not the time to be a hero, it's a market where you protect your capital." In particular, he's troubled by the Federal Reserve's mandate to raise rates. He said, "The market is going to humiliate the Fed."

Gundlach's advice for investors right now is to buy closed-end bond funds and real estate investment trusts, many of which are trading at historically low discounts to net asset value (NAV).

Buying a closed-end fund at a 15%-20% discount to NAV is "sort of a no-brainer," he said. Closed-end funds issue a set number of shares, so the price of that fund will rise and fall like a stock. And at times, extreme sentiment will send these funds to large premiums or discounts to their NAV.

In 2015, Gundlach purchased shares of mortgage REIT **Annaly Capital Management (NYSE: NLY)** yielding more than 11%.

Seth Klarman (Net Worth: $1.35 Billion)
CEO and President, Baupost Group

Since founding Baupost Group in 1983, Seth Klarman has returned more than 17% annually to investors. He has crushed the S&P 500. And more impressively, he achieved that feat while often holding 40% or more of his fund's assets in cash.

Klarman is a value investor. He looks for mispriced opportunities across all sectors of the market.

In his 1991 book, *Margin of Safety*, Klarman outlined many of his favorite investment strategies. The book is now out of print but copies sell for as much as $4,000 on Amazon.

Like many of the other names on this list, Klarman increased his firm's exposure to energy in 2015.

The $27 billion Baupost Group owns around 15% of liquefied natural gas company **Cheniere Energy (NYSE: LNG)**. Klarman also owns **Antero Resources (NYSE: AR)** and **Pioneer Natural Resources (NYSE: PXD)**.

Klarman's Baupost partner, Jim Mooney, wrote, "Although we are excited to see the credit markets coming our way, the opportunity [in energy] feels like it is just beginning to take shape. As always, we temper our zeal with patience and respect for the fact that we are, likely, in the very early innings of this game."

Michael Burry (Net Worth: $250 Million Est.)
Founder, Scion Capital

Though not yet a billionaire, you may recognize Burry's name from the Oscar-nominated film *The Big Short*.

Burry is a medical doctor turned investor who famously predicted the crisis of 2008 and made an estimated $100 million during that year.

In 2016, Burry said...

> The 2008 crisis incredibly made the biggest banks bigger. And it made the Federal Reserve, an unelected body, even more powerful and therefore more relevant. The little guy will pay for it – the small investor, the borrower. Which is why the little guy needs to be warned...

These days, Burry focuses on trading one thing: **water**.

In an interview with *NY Mag*, he explained why he feels so strongly about this investment...

> Fundamentally, I started looking at investments in water about 15 years ago. Fresh, clean water cannot be taken for granted. And it is not – water is political and litigious. Transporting water is impractical for both political and

physical reasons, so buying up water rights did not make a lot of sense to me, unless I was pursuing a greater fool theory of investment, which was not my intention.

What became clear to me is that food is the way to invest in water. That is, grow food in water-rich areas and transport it for sale in water-poor areas. This is the method for redistributing water that is least contentious, and ultimately it can be profitable, which will ensure that this redistribution is sustainable. A bottle of wine takes over 400 bottles of water to produce – the water embedded in food is what I found interesting.

One Final Thought

By Sean Goldsmith, Managing Director

It's time to take action...

You're already far ahead of most Americans simply because you read this book. You now know what some of the smartest men in the world are doing to protect their fortunes today...

Like Bill Bonner, who says the best place for your money in 2016 is in cash or gold.

Like Dr. Steve Sjuggerud, who sees an incredible opportunity in real estate.

Still, we're in the midst of the greatest financial experiment in history.

The Federal Reserve has printed nearly $4 trillion to boost the economy. And it cut interest rates closer to zero in hopes of stimulating growth.

Central banks around the world have followed suit.

Close to 30% of developed-nation sovereign bonds (more than $7 trillion) are yielding less than 0%. It's worst in Japan. Yields on 10-year government bonds went negative for the first time in history in February 2016.

What do negative interest rates mean exactly?

Simply, that people now pay for the privilege to loan the government money. Let's say you buy $100,000 of government bonds that yield -0.5%. You would pay $500 a year for the "safety" of holding sovereigns.

And despite all these efforts, the global outlook remains grim.

Growth is slowing, wages are stagnant, and commodities are crashing.

Quantitative easing took place to save the banks, right? But the Fed has failed by that measure, too...

Several of the largest European banks are now trading below their post-subprime-crisis levels. American banks aren't faring much better.

So central banks have failed at boosting the economy. And it seems the world is finally questioning their ability to manufacture prosperity.

We'll likely see another round of quantitative easing – QE4 – before it's all over. And as it has in the past, it will probably boost prices for stocks and other financial assets. But it will still fail to create any real growth. We predict this will be the final blow to fiat currency.

In Ernest Hemingway's *The Sun Also Rises*, one character asks another how he went bankrupt...

"*Two ways*," he replied. "*Gradually and then suddenly.*"

The same is true for banks... and nations.

We're currently in the "gradually" phase of our decline... Unfortunately, nobody knows when the "suddenly" phase will hit. But it will be swift and severe. That's why you must take steps today to prepare yourself.

Again, we cover some important concepts in this book. But there's plenty more you can do.

To stay up to date, be sure to follow Porter Stansberry's monthly publication, *Stansberry's Investment Advisory*. If you're not already a subscriber – or if you're having difficulty accessing your subscription – call our Baltimore-based Member Services team at **888-261-2693** and visit our website at www.stansberryresearch.com.

Best regards,

Sean Goldsmith
Managing Director, Stansberry Research

More From Stansberry Research and Our Friends

More Books From Stansberry Research

Dividend Millionaire
By Brian Hunt

The World's Greatest Investment Ideas
By Stansberry Research

Secrets of the Natural Resource Market
By Matt Badiali

World Dominating Dividend Growers: Income Streams that Never Go Down
By Dan Ferris

Doc Eifrig's Big Book of Retirement Secrets
By Dr. David Eifrig, Jr.

High Income Retirement
By Dr. David Eifrig, Jr.

The Living Cure
By Dr. David Eifrig, Jr.

The Doctor's Protocol Field Manual
By Dr. David Eifrig, Jr.

More Books From Our Friends and Colleagues

Living Rich: How to Live as Well as a Billionaire on a Middle-Class Budget
By Mark Morgan Ford

How to Speak Intelligently About Everything That Matters
By Mark Morgan Ford

Hormegeddon: How Too Much of a Good Thing Leads to Disaster
By Bill Bonner

Family Fortunes: How to Build Family Wealth and Hold on to It for 100 Years
By Bill Bonner and Will Bonner

Totally Incorrect: Conversations With Doug Casey
By Doug Casey and Louis James

Right on the Money: Doug Casey on Economics, Investing, and the Ways of the Real World with Louis James
By Doug Casey

Sword into Plowshares
By Dr. Ron Paul

End the Fed
By Dr. Ron Paul

The Revolution: A Manifesto
By Dr. Ron Paul

Liberty Defined: 50 Essential Issues That Affect Our Freedom
By Dr. Ron Paul